Pathway of Light

Pathway of Light

Poetry for the Soul, Volume 1

April Smith

iUniverse, Inc.
New York Bloomington

Pathway of Light
Poetry for the Soul, Volume 1

iUniverse books may be ordered through booksellers or by contacting:

iUniverse
1663 Liberty Drive
Bloomington, IN 47403
www.iuniverse.com
1-800-Authors (1-800-288-4677)

All scripture is taken from The Holy Bible, The Authorized King James Version

Cover photograph is a picture taken by the author on The Blue Ridge Parkway

ISBN: 978-1-4401-4530-8 (sc)
ISBN: 978-1-4401-4531-5 (ebk)

Printed in the United States of America

iUniverse rev. date: 05/14/2009

This book is dedicated to
Jesus Christ, Who saved my soul and
inspired me to write these poems.
Thank you, to my family, who was
supportive and patient with the much
time involved in putting it all together.
Thank you to my dear friend, who
encouraged me to publish them.
Thank you to the preachers,
missionaries and evangelists that I
have heard over the years, whom The Lord
has used to shape my and my family's life.
Thank you to my parents and siblings,
I cherish many memories of time well
spent together. Thank you for your support
through the years, with my writing.

Table of Contents

Chapter One

Pathway of Hope

Why are thou cast down, O my soul? and why art thou disquieted within me? hope thou in God: for I shall yet praise him, who is the health of my countenance, and my God.   Psalm 42:11

WHAT A BEAUTIFUL DAY

I used to use this expression on days that offered plenty of sunshine and clear skies

But, then, along came Jesus, Who saved my soul and opened my blinded eyes

Suddenly, I would arise thinking how great it is to be bound for Heaven

I'd exclaim, "What a beautiful day", as I focused on being forgiven

Soon storms and trials came, bringing sorrows and grief

But, my Lord taught me to still proclaim, "What a beautiful day", for I know The Prince of Peace

I read my Bible, while lounging around

And, I can't help but say, "What a beautiful day", when a new gem I've found

As I see souls converted, the old fashion way

My heart bursts with the praise, "What a beautiful day!"

I miss my dear brethren, as their bodies are placed in silent graves

But, I soon rejoice as I think about them walking the streets of Heaven, and I think, "What a beautiful day"

I often times imagine what it will be like to see my Saviour face to face

And, though it hasn't happened yet, I can say, "What a beautiful day", when I can thank Him for His amazing grace!

WOOL AND DUST, WEEDS AND RUST

I dropped some of my faith one day

And Jesus picked it up and brushed it off and gave it back to me today

I hadn't opened my Bible in so long, it had cobwebs and dust

But, today, I picked it up and cleaned it off

The flowers in the garden of my faith started to droop and be overcome with weeds

But, by renewing my faith in God, the flowers now stand strong, and the weeds have been
    removed through faith the size of a mustard seed

I was feeling my inner gears grinding and beginning to rust

But, today I felt those gears get serviced because I told God that in Him I will trust

The wool was pulled over my eyes

But, today He tugged it off, and I realized

That in my heart God is Number One

And with Him, another wonderful journey I've begun

He knows that my faith may not always be strong

But, He forgives when I ask, restores my faith and helps me along

HE HELPED ME THROUGH THE NIGHT

I've been so hurt that I cried myself to sleep, feeling as low as the dirt

I've been put down so much, that I begged God to bless me with His special touch

I've been lied on, cheated on, even spat upon, but by God's grace, I moved on

I've felt like a prisoner in my own home, crying to God to give me backbone

It's hard being emotionally abused, you feel as though you're walking on glass, not knowing
    what to say or do

It's hard being the victim of harsh, mean, cutting words; sooner or later, you lose all self worth

I've had times when I wanted to throw the towel in, and give up on everything, until God told
    me to do so is sin

How horrible it is to lay down at night, with fear and knots in my stomach, wishing for
    morning light

Oh, the times I've gone alone in another room, even in my closet, to kneel and cry to The Lord
    to save me from the feeling of doom

I've felt the very presence of satan yelling at me and pointing at my nose; I shuddered within,
    wishing he would just go

There are stains in my Bible where tears dropped, as I cried out to The Lord for wisdom,
    hoping this unfair treatment would stop

I've been the victim of a demeaning crime, too shameful to name; God helped me to forgive
    the one who was to blame

It seems like when terrible things happen, night time makes it worse; I'm thankful that God
    wraps His loving arms around me, and shares a special verse

Many times, having no shoulder to cry on, I'd cry in a towel to God, and then feel His tender arm

So many nights He has helped me through, without His comfort I wouldn't know what to do

Through His comfort, Word, and prayer, many nights I wasn't really alone, I felt Him there

The world would say that I have every right to be bitter, but I know better

I love my Lord too much to hold on to bitterness, and start a grudge

God says to do good to them that do you wrong, I've found the grace to do so and move on

Amazingly, He gives me the ability to forgive, wishing others no harm

He has turned my hurt by them into pity for them, causing me to easily forgive their sin

I might not be as close to my Lord, had others not pushed me into His arms

I wouldn't be able to tell YOU that He will help you, too, through the night, had I not needed Him to help me through the night!

I promise you that if you call on Him to help you in the night, He will still be with you come morning light!

Jesus does heal heart aches, He will answer when you pray, and He will be with you in the night, as well as the day!

The years are passing by, and hard hearts I've seen Him soften, I'm grateful that He has been with me each step of the way!

I can now say that it's been worth it all, I've learned that He is faithful; I'm more humble, and now, to others I can be helpful!

Resistance really does build strength, I've experienced this fact, at great length!

TINY FINGERS

We all love that heart-melting feeling of our finger being grasped by precious, tiny fingers

It touches us deep inside and makes our heart sink, and with joy, quiver

Whenever we're around tiny ones, we place a finger out for them to reach, hoping they'll grip it tightly

We don't force them to grab on, we sit there and wait patiently

No matter how big they get, they will still be "tiny" fingers to us

And, we will still yearn for that feeling as they grow; they are "gripping" if they are growing in our image and likeness

In the same manner, Jesus loves that feeling of our "tiny" fingers grasping on to His finger

And if we grab a hold, we will feel a joy so deep inside that we'll quiver

He is always holding a finger out for us to reach, hoping we'll grip it tightly

He won't force us to grab a hold, He just waits patiently

No matter how far in life we go, His finger will remain, for us to grasp; always just a reach away from us

And, He hopes that we may show others how to grasp, too, and stride to be in His image and likeness

UNDER THE SHADOW OF THE ALMIGHTY
BASED ON PSALM 91

Since I've been born again, I have a secret place to go
In times of grief, sorrow, discouragement, and in times of peace and joy, this place I know
No matter what situation life brings to me
It will find me in my Refuge, my Fortress, under the shadow of The Almighty
What a warm, comforting feeling, what peaceful assurance He brings
When He covers me with His feathers and I find myself under His wings
And if that isn't enough security for my days
I have the promise He gave that His angels will watch me and keep me in all my ways
For all life has to offer, there's no place I'd rather be
Than under the shadow of The Almighty!

IN THE MEANTIME, IT SEEMS LIKE SPRING TIME

It can be twenty degrees outside
With sleet and snow falling from the sky
As I sit, gazing out the window, I think about Jesus and I reflect upon the fact that He is mine
And, I find myself thinking, "In the meantime, it seems like spring time"

When things try to get me down
And satan tries to make me frown
I read some chapters in the Bible, and I thank Jesus for being mine
And, I soon am smiling and believing, "In the meantime, it seems like spring time"

Sometimes I'm not sure of what to do or say
And I don't want to behave wrong, because the consequences I'll pay
I am soon on bended knee, pouring out my heart, and I praise Jesus because His Holy Spirit is mine
And, as I patiently wait on an answer I praise Him, saying, "In the meantime, it seems like
    spring time"

At times I am persecuted for living for my Lord
I am threatened, put down, and so much more
But, when tears begin to swell, I stand confident because The Great I Am is mine
And, in the midst of persecution I have the attitude, "In the meantime, it seems like spring time"

In mountains high or in valleys low
Jesus brings a breath of spring time and I can feel the gentle spring breeze blow
When the roses smell dead, The Sweet Rose of Sharon fragrances the air
Because Jesus lives inside of me, is all around me...in fact, He is everywhere!

SOLID ROCK BOTTOM

Some of us are fortunate enough in life to come to a special place

A place in time in which we feel as though we're losing the game of life, and have no reason for
    wearing a smile upon our face

For, it is then that we turn to our Lord and beg Him to help

It is then, when we turn to Him, when we allow Him to show us what He's all about

Even though we haven't called on Him, until we lost all rays of hope

He gladly accepts our cries of desperation and shows us how to cope

If He is the last resort for us, this is when we put Him to the test

It is then, when we exercise our faith, that to us, He seems to do His best

The first thing He brings to us is the point of being humbled

And, after that, we become aware of the blessings we do have and are sincerely thankful

His next challenge is that we must truly believe

For, He shows us that the more we believe, the more we receive

And it takes many of us to arrive at the solid rock bottom

For us to realize that we have A SOLID ROCK to stand on!

MY ADDICTION

It's been a while now since I had my first dose

It wasn't pills, drink or drugs-it was The Holy Ghost!

You see, I met Jesus and He moved inside of me

Now, I look at everything differently!

I used to long for the peace that the world offers

But, since I've been saved I have more than peace, I have a Friend that sticketh closer than a brother!

He lives inside of me

He changes me daily!

I love to read His Word, sing Him praises and thank Him for His goodness

When I turn to Him, I can't help but forget about stress and problems!

I praise Him for the day He flooded my soul with conviction

Since that day, He is my addiction!

AT THE BASE OF THE MOUNTAIN

As we go through life, we'll face "mountains"

Most times, we are intimidated by the size of them

But, we know we don't face them alone, for, our Saviour lives within us

Suddenly, fear subsides and confidence arises

After all, He created real mountains, so what's a "mountain" of problems?

If it is His will, He can say, "be thou removed", and, it's gone

And, if it is not His will for it to disappear, it is His will for us to learn to trust Him, and
become more longsuffering, and draw yet more strength from Him, than ever before

So, the next time we're at the base of a mountain, we must pray

And, if the mountain is not removed, we ought to realize that it will work out for our own
good, and, through it all we'll learn to trust Jesus to get us through

At the base of a mountain, we should thank God that it's before us

Because each one is an opportunity for our faith to grow stronger, and for us to realize the
magnitude of God's faithfulness toward us!

ALL THAT REALLY MATTERS

When I find myself at the beginning of frustration, worry or fear

I soon am aware that The Lord is allowing it to come upon me, and I pray, and he dries up my tears

Then, I'm reminded that things will get better

Because I have Jesus, and that's all that really matters!

When I find myself in the midst of confusion, sorrow, pain or grief

I become aware that The Lord is allowing it to come upon me, and, when I depend on Him to
help me through, it seems to be brief

Then, I'm reminded that things will soon be better

Because I have Jesus, and that's all that really matters!

When I find myself in moments of happiness, joy and peace throughout my nights and days

I am aware that The Lord is casting it upon me, and I ask Him to listen for a while and enjoy
my feeble attempts of thanks and praise

And, I'm reminded that life isn't always going to be on the side of being better

But, I have Jesus throughout it all, and that's what really matters!

THE COLDNESS OF LIFE

In the midst of this cold, cruel world
Everyone seeks for arms of comfort, love and more
If you've never been saved, Jesus will speak to you
And, if you trust in Him, He will wrap His loving arms around you, and show you a love that's
     great, and true!

If you are already saved, and catch a chill from the coldness of life
Jesus will wrap His love around you, and remind you to let Him handle your problems and strife
When you consider life, and know the Giver
My friend, there's no need to shiver!

THE UNDEFEATED CHAMPION

My Hero, The Undefeated Champion is stronger than any force
He knows which way to go, when to everyone else He seems off course
My Hero, The Undefeated Champion has the power to move mountains
And, the energy He exerts in doing so doesn't weaken Him
My Hero, The Undefeated Champion has power to turn water into wine
And, He is mighty enough to see straight through your heart, as well as mine
My Hero, The Undefeated Champion carried my shameful sins, and yours, on His back and
     wore them as He hung on the cross
And, even then asked for forgiveness on our behalf, because He loves us
My Hero, The Undefeated Champion died and rose again
He defeated satan, and has the keys to death, hell and the grave around His neck, as He sits in
     His seat in Heaven
My Hero, The Undefeated Champion is my Saviour, my peace of mind, my only way to live
     forevermore!
My Hero, my Saviour is unconquerable, He is Heaven's Door!

SOAR AS EAGLES, CHRISTIANS

I was sitting outside today, on a picnic with my son
And, as we watched a hawk in flight, I made an observation
My son commented that the bird was not flapping his wings
And, I told him that he flapped already, and now, he's just soaring
This reminded me of what it's like as a Christian

We have to practice flying, in the beginning, by flapping

Once we take off, we need to flap our wings and learn how to go against the winds' currents

But, once we get high enough, we can soar, in any condition, under Jesus' influence

All Christians have the same destination, in which to land

But, it's impossible to get there without Jesus' guiding hand

My fellow Christians, I encourage you to be steadfast about your flight

And, baby Christians, I encourage you to flap with all of your might

Soar as eagles, Christians

And, it will be well worth it all, when we arrive at our new mansions!

IN THE STRENGTH OF JESUS

PHILIPPIANS 4:13 & 2CORINTHIANS 12:9

Only one begotten Son was manifested, to save us from eternal punishment

When God said He loved us, surely, that was something He meant

He sent His only begotten Son to deliver and teach us

Jesus obeyed His Father, because of His love for us He died on a cross

Any pain, hurt or emotion that enters our days

Jesus once upon a time suffered in the very same ways

Only, He could bear all the things that we cannot

He rose from the dead, and ascended to Heaven and left us Words, to never be forgot

When we observe our sufferings and our hurts

We should remember that Jesus had it much, much worse

If we turn over to Him the things we surely cannot handle on our own

He will give us help, like we've never before known

And, in the strength of Jesus, we find the grace to walk on!

BE HAPPY WITH YOURSELF

1TIMOTHY 4:14a

Neglect not the gift that is in thee...

Be happy with yourself

Know that God created you the way you are for a specific reason, and made you unlike anyone else

You may not yet be aware of the reason

But, grow in The Lord, and you'll find out in due season

He had something specific in store for each of us, when He made us

We should be thankful, and make no fuss!

FIRM GROUND

The devil tempts you enough to become low, and then he kicks you in the face, when you're on the way down

Please know that if Jesus is your Saviour, He will lift you back up and plant your feet firmly on solid ground

And, when you praise your Saviour for it, that devil won't want to stick around!

YOU ARE ALWAYS THERE

Lord, You are always with me, in the mornings so bright

You wrap me in Your loving arms, and then You bless me with peace each night

Lord, when the way seems dim, You always lead me with Your guiding light

Lord, You are always there, when others can't be found

You have a way of showing me that You're always around

Lord, You always leave me feeling protected and safe and sound

Lord, You are always there, to encourage and motivate me

You show me what to pray for, when I stand on bended knee

Lord, thank You for always being there, and for telling me You'll always be there, too, in my eternity!

SOOTHED THROUGH

There have been times in my life that I found it hard to press on

There have been times that I have been this world's victim, and was overcome by deception

But, in the midst of it all, the hand of Jesus was reaching out, for me to grab on to

So that He may soothe me through

No matter what situation I am ever in

Jesus' arm is always extended toward me, His hand anxious to feel mine grasp and hold on to Him

No matter how many tears are streaming down my face

No matter how much my heart breaks

If I call on Jesus, He soothes me through, and wipes away all of my tears

And eases my heart-aches and fears

I just don't know what I'd do

If I didn't have Jesus in my life to soothe me through!

CLOSE YOUR EYES AND SWIM

Sometimes the waters of life are murky, dark, anything but calm, and there are sharks all about

But, we must be reassured that our Lord will get us through, no doubt

Since we are His, He knows what is best for us

If we trust in Him, the waters won't seem so tough

And when we do feel that we are in scary, unstable waters again

We should call on Jesus, trust Him, and close our eyes to our problems and swim

The sea of life cannot be perfectly calm and shark-free

But, what gives us the motivation to swim on, is the promise of our Home in eternity

If we have Jesus, we know our destination

Jesus alone is the map that will guide us to God's glorious Kingdom

We can make it through any kind of waters, with Him

All we need to do is focus on Jesus, close our eyes to our problems, and swim!

TURN TO JESUS

So many times in my life, I made decisions, wrong ones

So many times in my life, I struggled with forgiving those who left me feeling hurt, sad, angry and even stunned

So many times in my life, I was too busy to notice my blessings

So many times in my life, I had fear in me about new beginnings

All this, UNTIL I turned to Jesus

He is Who teaches me how to make wise decisions and how to grant to others genuine forgiveness

And, after I turned to Jesus, I clearly saw all the tender things that I am blessed with

And, my sweet Jesus even took away my fears about change and newness, and He gave me instead peace, to carry within, as long as I live

Which shall be for all eternity

Because I turned to Jesus, He and His Father promise this to me!

FRESH ON MY MIND

I never know when an obstacle will pop out of time

That is why I always stride to keep Jesus fresh on my mind

If I study God's Word regularly

I will be able to see obstacles more clearly

For, if I keep Jesus fresh on my mind

With Him, I can overcome any obstacle that pops out of time!

HOW HARD IT IS

As a child of God, sometimes I pray and want an answer right away

How hard it is sometimes, to wait just one more day!

At times, I witness, and hope for immediate results to show

How hard it is sometimes to wait and watch the seeds grow!

In moments of discouragement and tribulation, I yearn for an untroubled day

How hard it is sometimes to look upon these moments and see that Jesus has reasons for
    allowing things to happen this way!

As I close out my every prayer

How hard it is to not hear Jesus say, "Fret not about tomorrow, for I AM already there!"

How hard it is to forget that He really cares!

A PACK OF WOLVES

If you were in the center of a pack of wolves

Wouldn't you look for a way out, for a hand to hold?

Well, problems in life resemble that pack of wolves

And I have found a way of getting out, when most would feel that there's no hope

No matter how many wolves are in the pack that surrounds you

Would you believe that there is always a hand strong enough to pull you through?

Well, the hand that I trust to grasp is that of Jesus...The only One that's true

And I know that He will always help me, because that's what He promised me He will do!

THANK YOU, GRACIOUS LORD

Lord, You have blessed me with so many of the things that I have prayed so hard for

I understand, Lord, the reason I had to wait so long for some of them to knock upon my door

You were preparing my blessings, Lord, and I had to go through what I've been through to
    appreciate them that much more

Lord, You have blessed me with better blessings than I ever hoped to some day own

Lord, You did this for me because of Your forgiveness and loving devotion

You waited for me to come to the point of being completely humbled, Lord, just so that I
    could realize where my blessings come from

Thank You, Gracious Lord, for Your blessings, forgiveness and so very much more!

YOUR MANY BLESSINGS

Lord, how come I oft times find myself beginning to grumble or complain?

Shame on me! Convict me, instead, to just praise Your Name!

After all, I'm still saved...

From the Book of Life, my name will never be erased!

Amen! Help me to praise You for Your many blessings upon me...

After all, today I have a place to call home, and plenty to drink and eat!

Lord, how come I oft times find myself discouraged, and shedding tears, in despair?

Shame on me! Open Thou mine eyes and let me never give up, because You're everywhere!

Let me remember that the God of Abraham and Jacob can still move in power this day...

After all, Moses and Your children came to the sea, You just moved it out of their way!

Amen! Help me to praise You for Your many blessings back then, which were recorded for me
    to find hope in, now...

After all, You brought all of them through, so surely You'll see me through somehow!

Lord, help me daily to realize Your many blessings, special for ME...

Help me to walk in the Spirit, and glorify You, instead of the bad things that be!

REVITALIZED

ENCOURAGED BY MRS. SANDRA OWENS

I gave God the biggest burden I'd ever faced in my life

And He gave me an abundance of His blessings last night

I was worried, anxious and stressed out, but this morning I find myself revitalized

My burden was so big, that I didn't want to bother asking God to handle it for me

But, I soon found that it was getting too heavy

Someone close to me reminded me that God wanted to help me, so I found myself in prayer,
    giving my burdens to God to carry

I hoped for results overnight, but a few days passed before He sent the answer, the blessing

But, it was more than worth the waiting

He didn't just take care of one of my burdens, He took care of everything

Last night, I did not suffer from spiritual depravation

The blessings God gave to me brought new hope, and much needed relaxation

And, this morning, I feel calmness instead of confusion and frustration

I believe that sometimes God waits until we completely give our burdens to Him

Before he lets particular blessings begin

I went to Him last, instead of first; I drained my spirit and strength trying to do it alone, but I have learned a valuable lesson

I have learned that He really is almighty, I used up all of my energy carrying my burdens around, but He took them when I gave them to Him, and He transformed them into blessings and gave them back to me

If that isn't praise worthy, full of love and power, then I do not know what is!

Next time something burdensome surfaces in my life, I don't even want to fuss over the details of it, I will just give it to our Lord

We cannot see Him, but we can lean on Him

We cannot see His ear, but if we whisper what we need, He hears and answers...

What makes it all possible is faith: believing that He'll take care of us, bless us, and be our Strength and Shield

I am forever grateful that He loves me and stays by my side

I've also learned that He expects me to give my burdens to Him, and He expects me to trust Him to handle all of my confusing situations

He has answered my prayers before...I guess I felt like I'd worn out my welcome out with Him, but unlike us, His love and gifts are never-ending

It is so exciting, knowing that He'll do this for me forever, if I only let Him!

MY JESUS

Sometimes I lose or misplace things, and it causes inconvenience

But, when it comes down to it, I just can't get upset, because after all, I still have my Jesus!

Sometimes, the tears stream down my cheeks as I go through times of sorrowful feelings

But, the tears soon dry up when the Holy Spirit within reminds me that I've still got my Jesus!

Sometimes, I get overwhelmed when I see those "fiery darts" coming...in hopes of breaking my heart into pieces

But, I am overcome with joy as I dress for battle, because I wouldn't have any armour to wear, if it weren't for my Jesus!

I can misplace things, experience sorrowful feelings, and feel satan's threat to break my heart to pieces

But, I easily overcome it all, when these five words ring in my soul, "I've still got my Jesus!"

GOD'S LULLABY TO THE SAVED

As infants, we all loved the comfort of being rocked and comforted by a lullaby

Something about it calmed our cry

Grown, we remember the technique

To help our little ones drift off to peaceful sleep

Although grown, we are still "babes" to God, our Father above

And He comforts us and offers us His lullaby of love

He cradles us in His essence, His Spirit

And plays a lullaby to our souls through His Word whenever we read or hear it

Just as any parent rocks their babe to sleep

God rocks His babes, including us parents, to a state of assurance about eternity

He did not learn this from us, but rather taught it to us

After all, God made us in His image and likeness

So, remember, as you comfort your babe, and wipe away their tears

That, at the same time, God is doing this for you, and will throughout all your years

As you hum your babe a lullaby

Listen for yours, from your Father, on High!

MY STRENGTH

I have a burden, too great to bear

The only way I'm onward pressing is the fact that my Lord's with me, the load to share!

Oft times, when I look back

I realize that it was God's grace, alone, that brought me through-for, He's never slack!

Although my burdens seem as though they could weigh me down

I'm always reminded that Jesus is holding me up, for, He's my backbone, the greatest strength
    I've ever known!

When I fall into tears and prayer

He comforts and consoles me and assures me that for all eternity, He'll be "right here"

I haven't any idea what I would do

If I had not the grace of God, in this life, to lead me through!

ALL I NEED

Although my supplies and resources may run low

Plead and beg-not me, because I still have all I need

Bible verses showed me what I needed for survival

A Lamb named Jesus Christ is with me every night and day

All I needed to do is open my heart to Him, and on His Name, call

I believed, and God's Son I received

I now live with His Holy Spirit living in my heart, and all that I need, He provides!

SEE IT THROUGH HIS EYES

Have you ever come to a point in life

When you could not see clearly, although you had open eyes?

No matter how much you strained or rubbed them, there was still a foggy haze

Surely you became frustrated as the haze thickened a bit more with each passing day

You were trying so hard to see it with your naked eyes

Then, you acknowledge that the Holy Spirit is reminding you how Jesus knows all, and you
    come to realize

That you can see everything with keen, crisp vision

If you simply go to Him

And pray to clearly see what the haze is trying to disguise

Suddenly, it is revealed, because you find yourself looking at it through His eyes!

MY PROBLEMS

God is not going to take our problems away from us

We have to give them of a free will

And trust that He'll

Handle them for us, if we give them with no strings attached

Just give the load of them to Him and walk away

And be reassured that He can and will conquer them, just because you showed true faith

I'm so grateful that our Lord works this way

And offers His help and many blessings to us day after day

HE'S ALWAYS WITH ME

It's another beautiful day!
Once again, I have so much to celebrate...
Jesus is holding my hand again today!

He touches me with His peace, and brings me inner-happiness, anytime, anywhere!
He always wipes away my tears and shows me how much He really cares...

By putting into my mind a thought of Himself hanging upon the cross...
So that I would not have to be lost...
In this confusing world that the devil is constantly raging across!

THAT'S NOT HARD TO DO

When the Spirit of Jesus spoke to my heart, pleading for me to be made anew
I saw my sinful condition, and as I trusted in Him, I thought, "that's not hard to do"
Upon being saved, He asked me to read His Word through
As I read through the pages, I said, "that's not hard to do"
When He shows me convictions that are new
His Spirit says to obey, and I answer, "that's not hard to do"
As burdens come my way, and satan cries out, "I'm going to hurt you!"
Jesus says that I should hide in Him, and I reply, "that's not hard to do"
When He says that I need to let Him guide my shoes
I am reminded that He knows what's best, and I think to myself, "that's not hard to do"
Jesus asks me to go to church each service, to hear His praise and truth
And, as I get ready, I tell Him, "that's not hard to do"
Sometimes, He tells me to sing in the presence of others, even though I can't sing in tune
As I'm reminded of all that He has done for me, I sing, "that's not hard to do"
When others are around, who do not yet know the good news
His Spirit tells me to share, so I proclaim, "that's not hard to do"
As I become weary, worn and discouraged, too
Jesus says that I need to press through in His strength, and I think, "that's not hard to do"
One blessed day, Heaven's pearly gates I'll pass on through
As I'm constrained to bow and sing praise, I'll say in my spirit, "that's not hard to do"
Then, my Saviour will say, "Follow me, to see the mansion I have just for you"
And, as I hold His hand, and stroll down the golden streets, I'll tell Him, "that's not hard to do"
Then, I'll add, "Thank You, Lord Jesus, and, I'm looking forward to spending eternity with You!"
"Now, that's not going to be hard to do!"

GOD'S STRENGTH

When my spirit is seeming low

I draw nigh to God and my strength grows

Every time I distance myself from Him, I know

Because self-pity, sorrow, vengeance, worry and anger begin to show

God always draws me to Himself, especially when I'm weak

And shows me that things aren't so bleak

Also, He teaches me how to, once again, become meek

FEBRUARY 22, 2001

The other day, in the early afternoon, my sun went down

Depression and anxiety slowly crept in, leaving be with nothing but a frown

A few days went by

But, thankfully, I realized

That I needed the Lord Jesus above

To touch my heart once again, with forgiveness to others and unconditional love

Today it snowed and iced, it is a gloomy day. But, to me, the sun shines bright once more!

Because I renewed my faith and trust in The Lord!

Every time I fall flat on my face

He gives me the strength to get back up and remember His grace

It's amazing how quickly He's already sending more blessings my way

And, It's amazing He does this after I was doubting Him just yesterday!

Thank You, Dear Lord, for helping me again

To be free from the pressures of this world that were leading me to sin

Once again, when I had a hard time believing in You

You were just a prayer away from showing me what I should do

Dear Lord: I cannot promise that I won't doubt You on another day

But I am grateful that You will never go away!

Thank You, God, for once again relieving me of all those feelings of anxiety and aggression

For taking away my feelings of being confused and in a depression

Thank You for letting me have another good day

And for directing happiness and peacefulness to flow my way!

SUN RISE

Have you ever watched the sun rise?

Would you agree that it is a marvelous sight to your eyes?

Are you ever amazed at the beauty it brings as it gradually fades out the night?

Have you ever noticed that the light pierces through little by little, until there is total light?

Although similar, would you agree that every sun rise is different and unique?

Each sun rise offers our eyes a different treat!

Have you ever noticed a sun rise from within your soul?

It only happens when you accept Jesus into your heart, and, of your life give Him control

Although I met Jesus at night

He created a sun rise within my soul that shed bright light!

And, when the sun sets in the sky, and darkens it completely

The sun rise that occurred in my soul sheds light continually!

WHEN LOST AND LOW, WHERE DO YOU GO?

When you are feeling lost and low

And you are confused as to which direction to go

Experiencing feelings of loneliness or grief

Although you see things, you still have doubt and disbelief

You feel like you're ready to give up trying

No matter where you are or who you're with, you bite your lip to keep from crying

When all the odds seem to be stacked against you

And you brainstorm, but cannot figure out what to do

This is a good time to open your door to Him Who is patiently knocking

To the One your mind has been blocking

Let The Lord in!

Just trust in Him and your blessings will begin

Believe in Him and show that you have faith

And joy, courage and strength, Jesus will bring your way

And the confusion you had about which direction to go

You will no longer have, because the answers He will show

All your sad and lonely feelings will begin healing

Those odds once stacked against you will turn into challenges you want to face

The sorrow and confusion inside you will be replaced

With love, forgiveness, peace and grace

That nobody can ever take away!

Just let Him dwell inside of you

Because His power, forgiveness and love is the only that is true through and through

He is the One you need to get in touch with

Because without Him, you cannot purposefully or eternally live

He is the only One you can completely count on and lean on to love you, guide you and show
    you the truth

No matter how many times you go aloof

He will always take you back if you start to stray

Thank Him for never turning us away!

I'VE BEEN ENCOURAGED

This ole' world has a way of bringing us down

Satan is always looking for ways to make us frown

We are persecuted, mocked, gossiped about, shunned and despised

But, my Lord said to me, "My child, it will be alright!"

Through a brother and sister in Christ, my Lord encouraged me

It helps to have brethren share a word of comfort and pray about the things that be

When reading God's Word, I've lifted my head, and my spirit proclaims, "I've been encouraged!"

And, suddenly, it all seems worth it

When in the gloom of doubt or despair

I've been encouraged, because the still, small voice of The Almighty whispered, "Be refreshed,
    my child, I'm with you, I'm not going away from here."

Oh, how I've been encouraged!

Oh, how my spirit has been lifted!

JUST ME AND YOU

Lord, as soon as You saved my wretched soul, You taught me a great truth

You said, "From here on out, it's just Me and you"

Saviour, I praise Your Name

For the salvation, to me, you brang!

Dearest Friend, as I sorrow, grieve and pray, not knowing always what to do

You assure me that You will take care of things, as You wipe away me tears, saying, "Until your
    answer comes, it's just Me and you"

Comforter, I lift and exalt Who You are

I praise You, Thou Son of David, The Bright and Morning Star!

Prince of Peace, as I reflect upon the past, I see me in the hour of need, with You guiding me through
I remember the scriptures You whispered to my heart, as You gave me absolute peace and told
    me, "I'm here, you're not alone -it's just Me and you"
Great Physician, You watched over me, and calmed my sickness with one touch of Your hand
How could I not proclaim and praise You throughout this land?

Soon Coming King, how I long for the moment I finally have a chance to humbly bow before You
I'll thank You, again, for all the times You whispered to me, "It's just Me and you"
Holy Lamb, my songs about You shall never come to end
You deserve to so be praised; therefore, I'll sing them over and over again!

EXPECT THE UNEXPECTED

My dear friend, don't grow weary or full of doubt
Remember that our Lord knows what this trial is all about
He has the tears counted, and, He will answer your every need and prayer
Stay close to Him, because He's the only One Who'll always be there
Though the days seem sad and the nights seem so long
Stay focused on Jesus, and He will make you strong
Find comfort in His Word, and joy in singing Him a song
It won't be long, and even this trial will be gone
All things are possible with God, our Father
He takes care of things like no other
Turn your face toward the sunshine, let your smile begin
And expect the unexpected once again
Though satan seeks to destroy you and bring you down
Rejoice in Jesus, and let go of your frown
Our God already has the victory, just believe and claim it, by faith
And be excited, because the unexpected may happen this day!

DON'T RUSH GOD

My dear friend in Christ, may I encourage you for a moment
Are you worn, tired, weary and spent?
Have you been waiting for a long time to hear an answer to a prayer?
Do you feel as though the answer will never be there?
Are you feeling like giving up hope, and moving on?
Have you forgotten how to keep holding on?

Do you feel like throwing your burden aside?
My friend, may I urge you to hold on with all your spiritual might!
The answer could be just moments away
If a miracle occurs, you'll surely think it was worth the wait!
Don't give up hope, friend, cling to Jesus, cling to hope
And, the answer you'll soon know!

SAVED

I am so thankful for being saved from the ultimate punishment someday!
But, also, I'm delighted about being saved in so many other ways
Not only have I been saved from a second death
Each day, with my every breath
I look around
And appreciate this new, happy life I've found
All life's dilemmas that come my way
With Jesus, I refuse to let them ruin my day
I have been saved from feelings of being unloved
Thanks to the amazing story of Jesus' love and giving me His cleansing blood
I have been saved from having negative thoughts toward tomorrow
It is so much easier to just give them to my Lord and not borrow all those unnecessary worries,
    stress and sorrow
With the start of each new day
I feel refreshed, because from so much, "I have been saved!"

PUSH, PULL OR DRAG IT IN

There is a popular automobile ad that states that we can push, pull or drag in our trade-in
No matter the condition, they guarantee acceptance, if we get it to them
They have us sign it over to them, and, in return, we receive a new one, but still need to pay
We know that the one we traded in was a worthless wreck, but, still, they accepted it because
    when it came to getting it to them, we found a way
I like to compare this with the grief we encounter throughout life
If we push, pull, or drag our trade-in to The Lord, our worry, pain, sorrow and strife
If we get it to our Faithful Lord, He will gladly accept it and send us on our way
And, what we get in return is a shower of His peace and comfort day after day
All we have to do is put our problem in His Almighty hands and let go completely

For, we know that if we leave Him, still holding on to our trade-in, that we are still needy

And we know that, if we leave with a smile upon our face, awaiting the shower of peace and comfort to fall

That the only payment we owe is to give Him the thanks, praise, recognition and glory for it all!

NOT A DREAMER, A BELIEVER

Because I learned the truth about God's Words and promises

Many people look at me, and others like me, and label us lost causes

Because I live for the things that are not of this world, people call me a dreamer

To you, I say, "if you labelers would read God's Word, too, you will understand that I'm not a dreamer, I'm a believer!

WHAT YOU CAN FIND IN JESUS

If you don't like yourself, ask yourself why

No matter what terms you use, it's because you need Jesus to fill you up, inside!

If you cannot find happiness

Trust in Jesus, and He will take away your sadness and replace it with gladness!

If you don't feel important to anyone

Know that if you fulfill your purpose, and witness about Jesus, you will become important to everyone

Because something you show or say

May change their day

In such a way, that they find their salvation, too

As well as eternal life-all because of the words they heard from The Lord, through you!

Find out what Jesus can bring in your heart

And then witness and you may lead others to their salvation!

You never know when it could be too late, so, you'd better pray for guidance, and then get started!

WHO IS JESUS

Just a prayer away

Every moment, night or day

Seeking to be our Rock and Defense

Unconditionally forgiving when we repent

Showing the world the only way to Heaven!

JESUS LOVES ME SO MUCH

Jesus gave His all-just for me!

He lived a sinless life, and suffered a cruel death on a rugged tree

He fought satan, and arose, in great victory!

He showed me the true way to Heaven-He delivered me from a devil's hell!

The smoke of my torment, no one will ever see or smell

And, I'm so happy about it, of all my joy, I could never tell!

Not only did Jesus save me, set me free, and change me by merely a touch

He showed me that He loves me so very much!

And, He told me to lean completely upon Him until I'm Home, that He will be more than
     just a crutch!

TOW TRUCK, PLEASE

Sooner or later, we all break down

And when this happens, we pray for help to come around

Some waiting periods are longer than others

Sometimes the longer the wait, the more thankful we are

No matter if it's a small repair or a major overhaul

One "Tow Truck" can take care of it all

No matter the weight

This One has the strength

He drives us to our knees

And gives to us peace

This "Tow Truck" has a driver, named Jesus

And His toll free number is 1-800-SAVE-US!

So, whenever I break down

I call the "Tow Truck" from out-of-town

And, I'll happily wait as long as needed

Because I know that nothing is too broken down to be saved by Jesus

There is never a fee to be paid

Other than thanks and praise

There is no minimum or maximum amount of uses

At the first sign of trouble, I just call on my Saviour, Jesus; And the stress fades quickly, because
     I have faith that He'll help me overcome it!

SECURED IN THE LORD

When tornadoes come along, what do we do?

Secure everything, so that the chances of things getting carried off are few

How about the big and little "twisters" of life, how do you endure them?

Well, the only guarantee of security, to withstand life's "gusts" comes from The Heavenly Realm

Trust in The Lord

Read His Word and pray daily, and, when the "twisters" come to town, you won't panic,
   because you know you're secured!

THINK OF JESUS

When I think I've got it rough

I think about Jesus!

When I think I'm victim of being judged

I think about Jesus!

When I think I'm feeling hurt

I think about Jesus!

When I think I cannot make a difference

I think about Jesus!

I can make a difference, by telling others the truth about Him!

What He did made a difference to every soul that ever has, now does, and will ever exist on earth!

When you feel "lost"

Know that you can completely trust in The One and only Jesus!

STARTING OVER

When structures collapse, they need to be re-built

We look to see what went wrong, and gather the new needed materials to rebuild with

If we are diligent and patient, exercising optimism

We can build a new structure, to be stronger than ever

Patience and wisdom are needed, much

It's not easy "starting over", but we MUST!

ONCE AGAIN

Here I am, Lord, once again
Here I stand, willing to confess another sin
Lord, as I "fess up", take my armour, and help me dress up

When I'm down in the valley, I realize the mistake I made on the mountain top
Forgive me, Lord, for up there, I take some of my armour off
It seems that I keep dropping my shield of faith
In Your strength, let me hold firmly to it each day

O God, help me to remember to prepare, on higher ground
Help me to be ready, before I'm on my way back down
God, help me to approach the valley prepared
And, remind me to search for The Lily that You put somewhere

Once again, Father, I started through a trial unprepared
And, once again, I allowed satan to cause me to despair
But, once again, I realize it and confess it to You
And, once again, You forgive and strengthen me, just like You promised to always do

So, my precious Saviour, I lift up my heart and voice to praise Your Name
And, once again, I thank You, that my condition CAN change
This time, Lord, I ask that You help me be ever ready for another valley
As I look around, from the mountains' peak, let me prepare for what I can't yet see

Once again, Lord, I ask You to help me stay focused on You, and on what's good
Once again, I ask for You to help my spirit be as it should be

THE JOY OF THE LORD IS MY STRENGTH

Dearest Father, please give me your ear
For, now I'm being tempted to despair
As I go through this trial, this dark time
Help me to stay focused on You, and let my light shine
Remind me, Holy Spirit, to realize all of my blessings, and to be thankful
Show me how to trust completely in You, and to continue being humble
Lord, help me to keep my mind stayed on Thee
Through all of these hard times, Your way, help me see
As I look into the mirror, let me see that You are still the health of my countenance
Help my feet to walk in obedience

At times, my faith is weak, so help me, Father, to daily dress in my armour

Remind me daily, to think on the day that I drank from The Living Water

Show me the wisdom I need, as I feast on Your Word

Lord, on the way, help me find others to serve

Help me to go forward, without looking back

Remind me that Your promises are not slack

Show me, again, Your power and majesty

Lord, as I stand still, a great wonder, let me see

Father, help my joy remain full, that You may receive the glory

And, as my joy becomes strength, help my lips share the story

Help my mind think on things that are virtuous, pure and good

Remind me to crucify my flesh and live as I should

Show my heart to praise Your Name as I walk through this valley

Lord, may I lead others to You through my words and by being a living testimony

Father, when the temptation to despair tries to pull on my heart strings

Help me to refuse and say, "the joy of The Lord is my strength"

WHAT FAITH IS LIKE

Faith is like a boomerang

When we throw it to The Lord, it comes back in the form of a blessing

Faith is like a key that unlocks a door

And, when we get inside, we find what we once prayed so hard for

Faith is like a fishing rod

And, when we cast it to The Lord, we reel in a blessing from God

A DAILY REMINDER

In order to receive the happiness of tomorrow

I must leave behind me today's sorrow

I need to fill up on the good, not holding the bad in

I must repent of my daily sin

I must remember that today is just a stepping stone

That I must step on to get closer to the bright, happy future I one day will own

GOD'S HAND

God is always reaching out His invisible hand
I cannot see it, but it always holds mine tightly and guides me
God is always holding out forgiveness for me to take from His hand
I cannot see it, but it means so much to me
God is always holding out consolation for me to take from His hand
I cannot see it, but it always comforts me
God is always holding out blessings for me to take from His hand
I cannot always see them, but I can always count on them
God is always holding out a promise to always love me, for me to take from His hand
I cannot see it, but it truly makes me happy
God is always holding out a shield to protect me for me to take from His hand
I cannot see it, but it always gives me security and safety
God is always holding out the comfort of His Son, Jesus, for me to take from His hand
I cannot see Him, yet, but He has touched my heart deeper than anything else ever can

God is always holding out an invitation to be saved, for lost souls to take from His hand
They cannot see it, but they should claim it this day!

TOO BLESSED TO BE STRESSED

INSPIRED BY MRS. WANDA TAYLOR

As I bowed low to pray, my spirit agonized within me
I found myself sinking into the depths of despair, no hope could I see
My eyes became fountains and my heart filled with fear
I was too burdened to talk to The Lord in prayer
My mind felt stressed and confused
So, I cried to God, "What do I do?"
His tender Spirit cleared my mind and comforted my heart
And, I felt satan's presence depart
My Father reminded me that I am still in His hand, my Fortress
Suddenly, I realized that there really was a silver lining in this cloud of stress
As The Lord dried my eyes, my spirit began to revive
And all those fears began to subside
The Holy Spirit told me to focus on Jesus, and to draw nigh to God
Quickly, I became thankful for the precious blood, of which I was bought
Hope came flooding my soul

For, now I recognized that God is still in control

His Word I'd hid in my heart started speaking to me

And I found myself no longer under the Juniper tree

Instead, I was under a rainbow, with blessings all around

Where the sin of doubt held me captive, grace did much more abound

I felt the sun shining on my face as I felt The Son shining in my heart

And as the breeze blew, I caught the scent of The Sweet Rose of Sharon, and then my praises
did start

Oh, I'd been too busy being burdened to notice the sun and feel the breeze

I overlooked so many of my blessings, until I came to God on my knees

Now, when the skies are gloomy, I search for some blue

And when clouds are thick, I search for the place where the light breaks through

When satan tells me that things are a mess

I take my Lord's advice and tell him, "I'm too blessed to be stressed"

Chapter Two

Pathway of Rest for Weary Saints

Come unto me, all ye that labour and are heavy laden,
and I will give you rest.   Matthew 11:28

MY LORD SAYS

In the mornings, quiet and refreshed

My Lord says, "Good morning, daughter." And, immediately, I'm blessed

To think that The Master and Creator of this universe says good morning to me is very
    exciting, I feel so unworthy

But, when He adds, "my daughter", I become thrilled and thankworthy

As the minutes and hours pass on by

I'm free to commune with Him Who sits on High!

My Lord says, "I have special time to fellowship with you!" This gives me peace and a spirit of praise!

To think that The Lord God Jehovah says He has time for even me gives me happiness that
    lasts for days!

While each day winds down, He is still with me

My Lord says, "Good night, child...as you sleep, I'll watch over thee."

To think that The Great I AM, He Who is The Alpha and Omega watches over me each night,
    I'm filled with comfort and confidence!

And, my Lord says, "My peace I leave you, for I am it's Prince!"

KEEP YOUR CHIN UP

My brother, don't look so sad when things go wrong

Listen to that Still Small Voice within, and praise Him with a song

Keep your chin up, way, high up

For, things don't seem so bad, when you're looking toward God!

My brother, don't feel so confused, and torn in two

Read The Word of our Lord, and He'll guide you down the path of truth

Keep your chin up, way, high up

And our Lord will show you the choice that will honor God!

My brother, don't be so discouraged and weary
Pray from the depths of your soul, "Lord, renew a new spirit within me!"
Keep your chin up, toward our Lord
And He will bless you with the courage and grace to endure even more!

NEVER DOWN TO STAY

When I feel burdened, and am bowed low down
Lord Jesus always brings me up, in His strength, and exchanges joy for my frown!
Ever since my salvation day
I'm never down to stay!

When I'm walking in a valley, and death stares me in the eye
Lord Jesus comforts me and pulls a praise out of a would be sigh!
He has shown me that come what may
With Him on my side, I'm never down to stay!

When I feel all alone in this ole' world
Lord Jesus reminds me, "I'm your Best Friend, forevermore!"
Even though I may walk that path, alone, the whole way
He lifts my spirit up, and says, "Rejoice, you're never alone, and when you feel down, know for
    certain that I have the victory for you, and you're never down to stay!"

ALWAYS POINT OTHERS TO JESUS

Dear child of God, there is an important fact you must know
We must direct others to Jesus, as we onward go
There are some who are lost
Child of God, you should point them to Jesus!

Dear child of God, we must encourage one another
We must do or say something to help, when we see our brethren suffer
When your brother or sisters' face is bowed low, in the dust
Child of God, you should point them, too, to Jesus!

It doesn't matter if others are rich, poor, big or small, nice or mean
Always point the lost to Jesus, to be cleansed and redeemed!
When your brother or sister is sad, in despair or doubt, when they say they've had enough
Always point them to Jesus to be comforted and for their spirit to be lifted up!

WORDS FALL FAR SHORT

One night Jesus spoke to my heart
And caused me to repent and be saved, and a new life start
I try to tell others about how I was transformed
But, my words fall far short

When Jesus led me to study The Bible
In my soul, I rejoiced because it finally made sense, after such a long while
I try to tell others what I learn from His Word
But, my words fall far short

When I hear a spiritual song, or a preacher preaching right
I shout and praise my Lord, because that gets me excited
I try to explain to others
But, my words fall far short

When Jesus takes me HOME someday
And I kneel at His feet to offer Him thanks and praise
I'll thank Him for looking at me and seeing His sinless blood applied to my heart
Only in my glorified body, will I be able to praise Him, without my words falling far short

How I look forward to that day
When I finally say exactly what Jesus wants me to say!
Until then, in this imperfect flesh and demanding world
I trust Jesus to make up for the loss, when my words fall far short!

LORD, WHAT WILL IT TAKE?

Lord, as You know, there's a heavy burden upon my heart for my loved ones
Lord, I beg of You to reach Your Holy Spirit to them, and tap on their hearts with whispers of
    true salvation
Jesus, I know You will come any day now
And, I pray that they'll accept Your gift, beforehand, somehow
Father, break their hearts
And show them that they're in "the dark"
Lord, use me, if it is in Your will!
Lord, if it takes me going back down into the valley, please let me do so, if that's what it'll take
    to get their eyes looking toward Calvary's Hill

Jesus, when my world was dark, You shone light, and led me to the path that leads to eternal
      life in Glory
Father, please let me be a light for them; I long for them, too, to be there, crying out with me,
      "For Thou Art Worthy!"
Lord, I'll fast, I'll pray, I'll sacrifice! Lord, what will it take...
For me to witness that they truly know You? Lord, help them no longer be deceived, religious,
      unknowingly fake!
Lord, I pray that they'll trust that You've paid their sin debt, too, and that their strong-holds
      will be broken; Lord, I wish they could be set free!
Father, I still pray for their souls, even if it means sacrifices and valleys for me!

A GOOD DAY FOR A MIRACLE

We all ought to daily keep our sins confessed
So that our days have potential to be extra God-blessed
We all ought to daily be purified and cleansed to the uttermost
So that our spirit will be filled with the fullness of The Holy Ghost
We all ought to seek to daily grow to be more spiritual
And, we never know what day our Lord could say, "This is a good day for a miracle!"

THE TEST OF FAITH

We know we have access to God, at any moment in time, through Lord Jesus
We know that all we have to do is call His Name, and He hears us
Sometimes, when our life seems calm
We find that our calling on Him is seldom
That is just the time that the devil is waiting for
To slip through the crack we've left at our spirits' door
This is when the devil does his best
To put our faith in our Saviour to the test
For, he thinks that if he can create reasonable doubt
That he can claim more of The Lord's "ground"
We must learn to constantly grow closer to our Lord, even when we feel as though we couldn't
      grow any closer to Him
Because the nearer we are to The Lord, the lesser the chance of the devil getting in
And, remember that if you find that you're having to test your faith
It's not that The Lord has left you; it's an insecurity the devil has created

So, stay focused on Lord Jesus and keep your faith strong; still claiming victory
And, you'll notice that your faith is strong enough to overcome satan's wiles, because it is
    placed in The All Powerful Lord, in God Almighty
The Lord may allow that devil to strip you of all that you have, and put your faith to a test
But, if you hold tight, in God's strength, and keep the faith and joy The Lord gives you, that
    devil will experience regret
Remember to grow ever closer to The Lord, and keep your faith in Him strong
Because, just when you ease up, the devil comes along

WHEN

When we start using words, referring to Jesus as our Saviour
We become comfortable with words like death, eternity, and Christian behavior

When we start using words, referring to our eternal Home
We become comfortable with words like funeral, rapture and final destination

When we start using words, referring to lost souls
We become comfortable with words such as witnessing, testimony and self control

When we start using words, referring to our enemy and spiritual wickedness
We become comfortable with words like Strong Tower, Grace and Faith; and we seek The
    Good Shepherd, our "Hiding Place"

ABSOLUTELY SECURE

People may think me odd or say degrading things about me
But that doesn't change the fact that I belong to Jesus, eternally!
People may persecute me, and say things that really aren't so
But, I'm in my Father's hand, and no one can pluck me out, for His Word let's me know!
People may not care about me, or even realize I'm here
But, that's okay with me, because my Father has counted my every hair!
People may say I have let them down, or that they think I've failed God
But, that's okay, Jesus knows my heart better than they, and when I repent, He assures me,
    "That, too, is under the blood!"
People may mistake my confidence in The Lord for self pride or self worth
But, that's okay, because I know and admit that there's nothing good about me, save the blood
    applied by my Lord!

Nothing or nobody can say that I am the same as before

For Jesus bought me and changed me, and because of this fact, I'm eternally, absolutely secure!

One more thing I must say is, "Praise, O praise I my Lord!"

My friend, if you don't feel absolutely secure, and can't praise Him, too, of your salvation, are you sure?

THERE'S ALWAYS A REASON

As a born again Christian, I have daily struggles and choices to make

There's always a reason to pray

Some more good reasons are all the lost souls I come in contact with each day

No one can ever convince me that there's not always a reason to pray!

As a babe in Christ, I daily face a new trial

There's always a reason to read my Bible

Some more good reasons are the fact that knowledge and wisdom, I need, for daily spiritual survival

No one could ever cause me to believe that there's not always a reason to read my Bible!

As a child of God, I am faced daily with things that lead me to enjoy my day

There's always a reason to offer praise

Some more good reasons are the facts that I'm saved, Heaven bound, destined to, with Jesus, always stay

No one could ever convince me that there's not always a reason to offer my Saviour words of praise!

FAITHFUL BURDENS

Some burdens, I believe, as a child of God I ought not bear

There are some that I must give totally to Jesus, and leave there

Other burdens, I believe, He puts within the depth of my soul

These are always pressing on my mind, heart and spirit, they're coming, but out of my control

They might be for specific souls who need to be saved

Or, they could be for "Christians" who do not Biblically behave

These, I call "faithful" burdens, because they just won't go away

I remember that tugging burden I experienced for so long was lifted when that person was saved

An important lesson, I've learned recently:

When The Lord gives us "faithful" burdens, we mustn't complain, but rather fast and beseech God constantly!

NO ONE KNOWS BUT JESUS

As I live day by day, upon this earth

I am faced with spiritual challenges, but am learning to value their worth

Yes, it is worth it all, to face a new trial

Because in each one I come out closer to Jesus, and even more glad to be His child

Only Jesus knows how much He's led me to grow

Only Jesus knows the grief behind each tear, and understands my sorrow

Although I have great Christian companions

Jesus has shown me that when it comes to understanding me the best, He is the Champion

In my moments of praise, reflection and peace

And in my moments of weeping, grieving and falling to my knees

Jesus is always there to carry me through and to receive my feeble words of praise

Though many may be all around, and my spirit yearns to "bust"

I'm reminded that no one really understands, no one knows but Jesus!

ALWAYS SOMETHING TO PRAY ABOUT

Jesus saved and changed me

Only could He cleanse such a wretch, and cause me to now see

Once He, in my heart, moved in

All sorts of great and interesting things began to happen

Old habits began to disappear, my perspective began to change

I started finding new things to be interested in; my life was completely rearranged

Things I once enjoyed, I now despise

And these lips are convicted to not stir up wrath, curse or lie

By the power of God, I have been made into a new creature

And, He is constantly convicting me to have more godly behavior

Many things He has shown and taught me

One is to look at this world, spiritually

Everywhere I go and everything I do opens doors for a chance to pray

He tells me to pray several times each day

I look around, and **through His eyes**, I see people in need of a Saviour, as I once was, not too
    long ago

I see people hurting, suffering, feeling lonely, I see "Christians" who seem to not ever grow

I see people serving Him, and then I see others compromising

He shows me to pray about anything and everything

And, when it's not anyone else, in which I find a need to pray for

He shows me to draw closer to Him than ever before

He shows me my needs and convicts me by His Spirit
He shows me when my "lamp" needs to be re-lit
Of this fact, I shall never doubt:
There's always something to pray about!

WITH GOD

There is never a job too hard for God to do
There is no prayer that He won't send an answer to
There is no wound that He cannot heal
There is no salvation that He will not seal
There is no bondage that He cannot break His children from
There is no work that He'll leave undone
With God, all things are possible
With God, His children have great potential!

A GUARANTEED ANSWER

Sometimes we pour out our heart before The Lord for hours
Other times, we say quick prayers as think on our needs, and those of others
We ought to pray with urgency and belief that we will receive an answer from Him Who sits
    on High
But, we must remember that we may not hear the answer until days, or even years pass by
God's timing is always perfect
He will never leave our prayers deserted
Dear brethren, we ought always to remember...
When we pray to our Father, we are guaranteed an answer
It may not be exactly what we expected
But, we will hear back from The Lord! None of our prayers are neglected!
And, if it seems as though we've waited forever
Remember that God, so oft times, answers not just what we yearned for, but better!

I'VE BEEN SIDETRACKED

Lord, You opened my blinded eyes, once again

You opened my heart and showed me something within

How embarrassed I am at what I saw

How saddened I am, as I stand in awe

Please forgive me for being so busy serving You, that somehow my fellowship with You grew less

Have pity and help my wretchedness!

Help me to stop my service for You when it interrupts my fellowship with You!

Let me thrive in Bible study, prayer and praise like I should...

Before I do all I would!

Thank You for helping me see I've been sidetracked...

Thank You for getting me back on track!

TAKE IT UP WITH MY DAD

You may judge me, mock me and persecute me

You may put down my convictions, and doubt that Jesus gave them to me

One thing you must know is that I make no apology

Jesus saved my soul, set me free, and is constantly convicting and changing me

The mind and heart I used to have

Have been transformed, and of this fact, I'm glad

And, if you have a dispute or negative word, just take it up with God, my "Dad"

He's The One Who helps me choose between what's good and bad

Anything that will take me away from Him...

Anything that competes with my time with Him...

Anything involving ungodliness or abominations...

Count me out, 'cause when it comes to a choice, I choose Him

Anything short of that choice is a sin

So, take your comments about me to The Lord Jesus Christ, AMEN!

MY TOUR GUIDE

I enjoy going on tours

And, I am always impressed with the knowledge and information the tour guides deliver

They are obviously well trained

And, lots of information, they obtain

To disperse among us, as we follow their lead

We step where they step, in hopes that we'll see what they point out to us, with ease

But, sometimes, a question is asked, that they cannot answer

And, we are left to wonder...

Well, I have met one "Tour Guide"

That tours me through life...

Pointing out wrong from right

And tells me the answers I seek, by shedding His Light

He knows what answers I need to hear

Before my questions even appear

I don't have to guess where to step, to see life from His perspective, His "tracks" never disappear

And, I don't have to worry about being at the front of the line to get all of the information; for,
    His Voice speaks, and within my heart, I can hear!

I'M STUBBORN

1CORINTHIANS 15:58

Going through life, I try to keep an open mind

The Lord constantly shows me His ways, and convicts me to leave my old ways behind

If you've got something that, to me, you want to show

I'll sit and observe what you know

I'll give you a fair chance

I'll be "objective" as I listen and glance

But, one fact, you need to know...

If it is not going to glorify The Lord Jesus Christ, I'll try in His strength, not to give in, because
    His Word commands us to be stubborn when it comes to serving Him, The King of Kings!

THE UNSEEN

The most precious sight I've ever seen
Cannot be seen with the eye
I see through believing

The most powerful feeling I've ever felt
Comes from what I cannot see

It's very simple to explain,
I can sum it up by naming one Name:
Jesus Christ!

THE BACKSIDE OF GOD

So many people mean well, and pray to God for various things
And, they get disgusted, when a miracle or an answer He does not bring
They wonder why they only see the backside of God
And, whatever route they go, to try to see His face, they feel as though they've remained in the same spot
Christian, tell these needy people that Jesus Christ is the only Mediator for us
Tell them that God cannot look upon our faces, if we first haven't come to Jesus, to be made righteous
Tell them that they must believe in Jesus' shed blood, and be born again, and to then pray in His Name
Tell them that only then will God look upon them and listen to their prayers, when Jesus pleads, "It's okay to look and listen, Father, they're under My blood; they no longer pray in vain."
Christians, we must share the truth with these needy people, so that they may see The Face of God one day
Tell them that all they have to do is put their faith in Jesus when He invites them to, and yield to Him, as He continues to lead the way...

HE'S WITH ME ALL THE WAY

Lord Jesus saved my soul and made me white as snow

I'm enjoying living "under the blood"; my salvation is secured, I know

Jesus has been my Best Friend since I was first born again

There is no one who could ever compare to Him

He feeds me through the milk of His Word

He listens each time my heart gets stirred

Jesus hears my prayers, and knows my hearts' deepest desires

He's with me each morning, at noon, and each evening as I retire

He's there when I don't know what I should do

He shows me which path I should choose

Jesus has comforted me and calmed me countless times

Praise His Holy Name! I'm so glad that I am His and He is mine!

There's never been a day since I've been saved, in which I couldn't say:

He's been with me all the way!

Chapter Three

Pathway of Praise

O come, let us worship and bow down: let us kneel before the
Lord our maker.   For he is our God; and we are the people of
his pasture, and the sheep of his hand.   Psalm 95:6-7

YOU, LORD

You, Lord, are awesome, You, Lord, are great
You, Lord, deserve all glory, honor and praise
You, Lord, created this universe, and all that is within
You, Lord, deserve praise without end
You, Lord, are full of mercy and love
You, Lord, are so kind to visit lowly man, from above
You, Lord, show grace to those who are not deserving
You, Lord, look on our hearts, and are quick to be forgiving
You, Lord, are a Mighty Fortress, a Strong Tower
You, Lord, have all dominion and power
You, Lord, make the best promises, and keep each one
You, Lord, befriend folk that have none
You, Lord, are the only source of strength, joy and hope
You, Lord, give grace, so that we may cope
You, Lord, keep hungry souls fed
You, Lord, are Saviour, God and King
You, Lord, make my souls' joy bells ring
You, Lord, are my Rock, Shield and Comfort
You, Lord, are far above every other
You. Lord, are Wonderful, Marvelous, Magnificent, Full of Wisdom
You, Lord, are a Great Judge and Ruler of Your Kingdom
You, Lord, gave us Your Son, Spirit and Word
You, Lord, deserve to be worshipped by all the earth
You, Lord, are so gracious to look upon me, and incline Your ear to my every prayer
You, Lord, amaze me with how much, about me, You care!
You, Lord, deserve the best from all of Your children
You, Lord, deserve an eternity of praise from all of Heaven!

41

LOVE, AWE AND REVERENCE

Lord Jesus, my Saviour, in Heaven above

First, let me tell You about my greatest love...

When You saved my soul from hell, and wrote my name in The Book of Life

You put a deep peace in my heart, and assured me that You will handle even my future strife

You loved me so much, You gave all You could give

That's why I love You so much, and praise You for giving me eternal life!

Saviour, Creator, I stand in awe at Your creation

When I look at mountains high in the clouds, or at lily filled valleys, below, I'm reminded that
    my Father made them!

Lord of my life, soon coming King, I have for You the utmost reverence...

The reverence I have for You leads me to praise You, worship You, and stride to have more and
    more obedience to You!

Jesus Christ, Rock, Redeemer, my Saviour and Friend...

I cannot help but have love, awe and reverence toward You, 'til the end! AMEN!

INCREDIBLE NAMES

When I think of my Saviour and Lord

Many Names for Him flood my heart and soul

I think of Names such as The Great I AM, Master, Mediator

He's The God of all Comfort, my Rock, my Redeemer

Jesus is my Anchor, my Hope, my Joy, He is The Bright and Morning Star

He's my Refuge, my Fortress, the health of my countenance, the "Bestest" Friend I've had-by far!

He is my Salvation, The Author and Finisher of my faith, He's The Good Shepherd, The Only
    Begotten Son of God

Jesus is The Alpha and Omega, The Beginning and The End

When I think of Him, how can my praise find end?

He's The Great and High Priest, The Great Physician, The Word, The Door

Jesus Christ is The Soon Coming King, and praise God, I'll be with Him forevermore!!

JUST PLAIN AWESOME

I have a Friend...

He'll be with me still, after this life here comes to an end

He put the sun, moon, stars and planets in place...

He calls me His own, because I've been saved by faith through His grace

He is so Righteous, Majestic and Holy...

And He is Master, Saviour and Father to me

I adore how Great and Wonderful He is, I bow to worship The Lord of all creation...

He is Just Plain Awesome!

SWEET JESUS, ONLY YOU

Sweet Jesus, only You could save my soul from hell...

Only You could give me water from The Everlasting Well!

Sweet Jesus, only You could give me life anew...

Only You could change me through and through!

Sweet Jesus, only You can calm the storms within me...

Only You could give me Your Holy Spirit to guide me through all eternity!

Sweet Jesus, only You are there, when the world turns away...

Only You can bring me true joy on an otherwise "bad" day!

Sweet Jesus, only You do I wish to meet...

Only You, do I want to rush to, when my feet finally walk upon Heaven's golden streets!

Sweet Jesus, only You deserve the praise...

Only You will be Heaven's King, lighting up Heaven with Your glorious "rays"!

CAN'T GET YOU OFF OF MY MIND

Everywhere I go, and in all things I do...

I can't help but think about You!

You're in my mind, heart and soul...

My thoughts of You overflow!

When I need help, You're always there...

You know all about me, from my heart's deepest desire, to my every prayer!

You are so good to me, and mean so much to me, all the time...

Jesus, Saviour, Rock, Redeemer, Comforter, Great I AM, no wonder why I can't get You off of my mind!

ALWAYS A SONG IN MY HEART

I love those old gospel tunes
Because, Lord, they exalt and bring praise to You
But, none of them can ever compare
To the song You put in my heart, that is with me all the time, everywhere
I'll always remember when Your song in my heart did start...
And, I praise You, Jesus, because with You, there's always a song in my heart!

AGAIN AND AGAIN

Jesus, I'll thank You again and again for salvation
Saviour, I'll thank You again and again for all of my blessings
Lord, I'll thank You again and again for Your love, so true
Comforter, I'll thank You again and again for cheering me when I feel blue
Son of God, I'll thank You again and again, because of Who You are
Great I AM, I'll praise You again and again, because You are truly The Bright and Morning Star
Lamb of God, I'll praise You again and again, because you deserve all of my praise
Soon Coming King, I'll praise You again and again, throughout all of my eternal days

BECAUSE OF YOU

Lord, because of You, I'm forgiven
It's because of You that I'm on my way to Heaven
Lord, because of You, I'm a new creature
It's because of You, that I'll have a "bright" future
Jesus, because of You, I have sweet peace
It's because of You, that I'm heard, each time I'm on bended knees
Saviour, because of You, my lips proclaim salvation
It's because of You, that I'm a "missionary" in this "corner" of the nation
King of Kings, because of You, I'll bow at Your feet one day
It's all because of You, that I'll lift up my voice with worship and praise

SOUL EXCITEMENT

It's exciting to me, to see loved ones and friends
It's exciting to me to see newly born babies, puppies and kittens

Something about holding and looking upon the young brings excitement to me

But, that excitement only sinks as deep as my flesh, leaving me thirsty

Lord, that kind of excitement fades away...

When I'm with my brethren, and they exalt Your Holy Name!

Sure, I get excited when I see a newborn baby, a puppy or fuzzy kitten, and think of how cute they are

But, Lord, I find excitement within the depths of my soul, when I take a moment to consider their Awesome Creator!

Lord, nothing comes close to exciting me in the ways that You do

My soul wants to burst with excitement at even the very thought of You!

O LORD, I TRUST IN THEE

Father, my Father, Lord of creation

Only You can I always count on!

I trust in You, though the mountains crumble and fall into the depths of the sea

Thank You, Lord, for the very faith You gave me to trust in Thee!

Lord, O Lord, my precious Saviour

Only You can take someone so wicked and vile and change their behavior!

I thank You and praise You for opening my blinded eyes, causing them to see

Blessed be Your Name, forever, be Thou exalted and magnified, for Thou alone are worthy!

My Redeemer, my Rock, my Mighty Fortress

Only You could give me such confidence and boldness!

Thank You that in the midst of a battle, I can, through You, claim the victory

O Lord, I trust only in Thee!

THANK YOU, JESUS, FOR ALL YOU'VE DONE FOR ME

Jesus, You suffered shame, and defeated death

To You, I owe my every breath!

Jesus, You found me where I was, at just the right time

To You, I owe the rest of this life I call mine!

Jesus, You moved into my heart and changed my life

To You, I offer praise for exchanging joy for my strife!

Jesus, You give me the strength to make it through each day

To You, I give my will, show me the way!

Jesus, You alone know all of my grievances and burdens, and hear my every prayer

To You, I offer thanks for always being there!

Jesus, You give me hope, whenever I think about going into eternity

To You, I say, "Thank You, Jesus, for all You've done for me!"

AMEN, HALLELUJAH

Amen, Hallelujah to the wonders I've seen!

Thank You Lord Jesus, for Your Spirit so keen!

Amen, Praise The Lord for the souls recently saved!

Thank You, Lord Jesus, for redeeming them, too, from the power of the grave!

Amen, Hallelujah to the preaching I've heard!

Thank You, Lord Jesus, for my soul being more than just stirred!

Amen, Praise The Lord for giving us The Word!

Thank You, Lord Jesus, for keeping Your Word preserved!

Amen, Hallelujah! My soul does rejoice!

Praise The Lord Jesus, for leading others to make the right choice!

To God be all glory! How I love His Sweet Name!

Amen, Hallelujah, to Lord Jesus Christ goes all praise and fame!

THANK YOU, HOLY SPIRIT

Lord Jesus Christ, I praise Your Name

Thank You so very much for the salvation, joy, peace and eternity I now can claim!

God, my Father in Heaven, how I love being Your child

Thank You for giving me Your only begotten Son, so that You and I could be reconciled!

Creator of all creation, I praise You, I praise Your Holy Trinity

Holy Spirit, how could I have ever been saved, had You not convicted me?

Holy Spirit, You drew me to my Saviour, and Father, yet, You are the Same as They

Holy Spirit, thank You, for showing me the right way!

Holy Spirit, thank You, for dwelling inside of an ole' sinner saved by grace, like me

Holy Spirit, thank You for always speaking to me and showing me how I ought to be!

Father, Son and Holy Spirit, thank You, from the bottom of my heart

Thank You for searching for and finding and saving and continually changing me! And I thank You for never being too far!

I love You! I praise You! I worship You! You are so righteous and holy

Yet, You took time for lowly me!

Thank You! Thank You! Let my lips always praise You!

Without my Father, Saviour and The Holy Spirit, I wouldn't be saved, changed or looking forward to eternity- to worship Jesus, The Door, The Way, The Truth!

Chapter Four

Pathway of Remembrance

My soul hath them still in remembrance, and is humbled in me. This I recall to my mind, therefore have I hope. It is of the Lord's mercies that we are not consumed, because his compassions fail not. They are new every morning: great is thy faithfulness.   Lamentations 3:20-23

I'M SO GLAD I KNEW IT WAS YOU

Lord, the night You showed me I was lost, and in desperate need of a Saviour...
Your Holy Spirit showed me that all I owned was an empty profession; convicted, I trusted in
    You , alone, and, immediately, You began changing my outlook and my behavior!
You showed me to truly repent of my sin...
And, You washed me up and gave me peace deep within!
Something told me that I needed to be born again, something changed me, in minutes, few...
It was unlike any previous spirit calling, I'm so glad I knew it was You!

All of a sudden, the words in my Bible started to become understandable and clear...
I now had discernment and convictions, and, I felt You ever near...
Something told me to study the Bible, so Holy and true...
I'm so glad I knew it was You1!

All of a sudden, my perspective changed...
And people told me that I was acting strange!
My desires were different from the ones I had before...
And, when I found Your wisdom, I sought after more!
Something made my life seem totally new...
I'm so glad I knew it was You!

When trials started, I had a different place of comfort...
And, You were enough, I didn't have to turn to any other!
Something told me that You're my Shepherd, my Friend, my peace through and through...
I'm so glad I knew it was You!

Each time satan comes, in hopes of confusing me...
I get on my knees and pray that You will help me be the best Christian I can possibly be!
One Voice stands out from all the rest, telling me what to do...
I'm so glad I know it's You!

Any day now, I'll be raptured into a new place...
And, I'll burst with joy as I finally look upon Your face!
I'll be so thankful that You didn't give me one life to live...but, rather, two...
As I pass through the clouds to be with You in the air, I'll cry out, "Lord, I'm so glad to know it's You!"

EYES RIGHT

I AM STILL LEARNING LESSONS FROM THREE AND A HALF YEARS IN ARMY JROTC, AND BEING IN THE COLOR GUARD AND ON THE DRILL TEAM

I was in Army JROTC for three and a half years
And I was taught history, obedience and discipline there
I joined the Drill Team and the Color Guard
And spent my Senior year as a Senior Officer
I took pride in my uniform, always sure to polish my boots and brass
I felt so dignified in being a member of such a unique, orderly class
I learned to give speeches, take commands, the chain of command
And, supported the cause, which is to serve and protect our people and our homeland
I enjoyed drilling in front of youngsters and others
In hopes that they might consider becoming my new "Army sisters or brothers"
I was honored each time I marched with and presented the flag
I felt as though I was respecting it, I wasn't doing it so that I could just boast or brag
And when we would have a drill meet or inspection, a command would be given when the
    officers and the American flag came to sight
Our captain commanded us by shouting out, "Eyes right!"
Out of respect, we turned our eyes to the right, and looked upon the flag as we continued to
    march on
And, as each of us came before it, we saluted it, to show that we're proud to be in America;
    honored to belong
And when our squads came to that predetermined spot
Our leaders ordered us to "halt"
We would stand tall and proud, waiting for the Inspectors to come and look us over and
    question us

And, if we weren't presentable or could not answer their questions we were still scored, with no
  ifs, ands or buts

Although we stood together and marched with others surrounding us completely

We were inspected individually

We gave each other encouraging eyes as the Inspectors made their way through

We were hopeful to pass inspection, and for all the others to pass, too!

As we waited for the final results, we tried to not lock our knees

And we each gave a sigh of relief when our Senior Instructor exclaimed, "We've passed...
  Company At Ease!"

I like to compare these memories to my Saviour

I find great similarity in my Army and Christian behavior

Instead of boots and brass to polish, I polish my character

And, I constantly ask myself if I look like a Christian to every other

I feel dignified in being an Ambassador for Christ

I willingly represent Him, as He willingly laid down His life

I enjoyed learning His chain of command

It's so simple, my Superior is The Son of Man, the blemish free Lamb

I absolutely support His dear cause

I happily accepted what He did for me on Calvary's cross

I will march wherever He leads me

And try to show everyone I meet how to accept Him and live humbly

And I am thankful that when I'm not sure of how to handle a situation, I have The Holy
  Ghost inside

Reminding me that the throne is nigh, and commanding me, "Eyes Right"

For, if I go through my life with my eyes to The One sitting at the right hand of The Father

I will remain focused and obey no other

And, on my final day, the books will be opened, and I will pass inspection

Simply because I turned my eyes right and accepted God's gift of eternal salvation

And, I look forward to passing into the Kingdom of The Lord, and being commanded, "At Ease"

And remaining "At Ease" for all eternity!

AS SOON AS I WAS SAVED

When The Holy Spirit of God beckoned with my soul

The Lord of all creation showed me that I was on the verge of hell

He showed me the wicked sins and filthy condition in which I was living

Then, He showed me the love of Calvary; The Lord Jesus, for me, bleeding

He told me He arose in great victory

And, He pleaded with my soul, that He did it all for me

I was gloriously born again the instant my soul yielded trust in Him

At that instant, I finally understood what it meant to be a Christian

As soon as I was saved, angels rejoiced in Heaven

Jesus told me I am now a member of His Royal Brethren

Though my sins were as scarlet, not they are gone, I'm washed as white as snow

My name was quickly written into The Lamb's Book of Life, I am no longer God's foe

My soul thirsted to know God in fullness

My spirit longed to be in obedience

My perspective began to change completely

I no longer desired to sin, not even discreetly

The Word of God started making sense, it was now more defined

I started looking at trials as a chance to be more and more refined

As soon as I was saved, I was changed

Second Corinthians, five and seventeen is my testimony, in God's Word, portrayed

Though I am far, far, far from perfect

I thank Jesus for covering me in His blood; He showed that His love for me was worth it

As I grow each day

I am reminded of the joy that came to me the moment I was first saved!!

A JOURNEY WITHIN

I frequently go on a long journey, inside

I travel to Calvary; the place where my Jesus suffered as He hung and died

I always get there just in time to see the whole sorrowful scene:

First, I notice a crown of piercing thorns embedded into His scalp

And, then, I watch the stakes being hammered through His loving hands and beautiful feet, and, I notice that He doesn't ask anyone for help

I noticed the dried saliva all over His body, where the soldiers spit upon Him

And, I noticed His perspiration, mixed with His blood; from where they whipped His flesh, tearing off His skin

Next, I watch as they erect His cross, and the crosses of the other two men

And, I hear Jesus say, "Father, forgive them; for they know not what they do."

And, then soldiers mock Him by writing above His head, "This is the King of the Jews"

One of the crucified men suggests that Jesus save Himself, as well as them

And, the other admits that they deserve it, but that Jesus doesn't, and he says to Jesus, "Lord, remember me when thou comest into thy kingdom."

And, Jesus replies, "Verily I say unto thee, To day shalt thou be with me in paradise."

And, around the sixth hour it becomes dark, before my very eyes

And, three more hours pass, before Jesus' last words, which were in such a loud voice, a cry, loud enough for many to hear it

He says, "My God, My God, why hast thou forsaken me?...It is finished..." as He bows His head, crying out, "Father, into thy hands I commend my spirit..."

Then, He gives up the ghost

And, this saddens me, yet, brings me joy to know that He died in my place-that strikes my heart the most

After each journey to Calvary, within

I find myself glad He still lives, and, I fall on my knees, repenting and confessing my recent sins

I will never pray to any other

Because I know what Jesus did for me at Calvary, so that I may stand redeemed, in the presence of my Almighty Father!

THE GRASS THAT IS GREENER

For as long as I can remember, a saying has been around

It is, "the grass isn't always greener on the other side"-but, one exception I have found

In this world, so dark with temptation and sin

It is so easy, to look to other pasture, and feel it's glory light me within

I followed the path that this light shone for me to travel upon

And, I found myself on a hilltop, called Calvary, the one that Jesus died on

Next, I came to realize that He suffered, died and arose so that I may come to the only place where the grass is greener

After I visited this remarkable place, I was sent back into my life

But, now that I know where this place is, where the grass is greener, I can easily pass on by other appealing pastures, knowing that those aren't even green compared to the pasture of Christ!

And, I am so excited about going to this place

That I will tell others about it, as I meet them on the way, by handing out tracts, or speaking face to face

BLOOD COVERING

I gladly give up my own righteousness

To accept the blood from The Saviour Who forgives and saves me, when on His Name I call, and my sins I confess

All I need to be saved is to receive His blood covering

The faith He gave me is the only payment I need to bring

I'll happily receive my salvation, through faith in His soul cleansing blood, shed at Calvary
I'll bathe in it, and become a new creature
And, change for the world to see
I'm glad His blood covers me, and that He convicts me to spiritually mature
I am thankful for what He did for me, coming to be our Saviour, in the form of a human
I cannot comprehend what He must of went through, as far as physical pain
However, I am grateful that He paid my sin debt in full, by shedding all of His blood that I
    may have a blood covering
I rejoice at the fact that when the Book of Life is opened one day, in it will surely be my name!

MY LORD IS SO PRECIOUS

I never gave a thought to the idea of seeing Jesus' face
Until the moment He reached out His hand and saved me by His amazing mercy and grace!
My Lord is so precious to me
He showed me how He suffered and died for me on Mount Calvary!

I thought, as I looked upon my new born babe, that I'd never have that much love toward another
Until Jesus introduced me to Himself, and, my Heavenly Father!
My Lord is so precious to me
He showed me the greatest love of all, by sacrificing His own body!

I thought my good works would get me into Heaven one day
Until Jesus showed me that He, alone, is The Truth, The Life, The Way!
My Lord is so precious to me
He bore my sins, saved me and set me free!

I thought I had my life all planned out
Until Jesus saved my soul, and showed me what life really is about!
My Lord is so precious to me
He saved me, and changed me, for the world to see!

I thought I could read my Bible through one time, and have nothing left to know
Until Jesus told me that if I read it again and again, He always has a new meaning, to me, to show!
My Lord is so precious to me
He showed me that I can never tire of reading His Word, and practicing Christianity!

I never thought I could be so homesick for a home in which I've never been to
Until Jesus told me, "I'll be there to greet you, and I have a mansion from Me to you!"
My Lord is so precious to me
I look so forward to kneeling before Him, and praising Him for all eternity!

REMEMBER WHEN

We all come to a point in life, when an experience we come to changes us

Something occurs and we sit in awe that we've just experienced something miraculous

Whether it be the unexpected recovery of a sick loved one

Whether it be the first time we ever held a new born

Whether it be the first time of anything significant that we experienced happen

We all have the familiar saying of "I remember when"

It is good to remember the things that changed us in just one split second of time

We are different because of that special moment; without even trying

It's amazing to me, how our perspective can change in an instant

Causing everything around us to seem to be different

I have lots of sweet, "remember when" moments to reflect on now and then

But, my dearest and most meaningful one is when I opened my heart to Jesus and invited Him in!

That moment changed me the most

That moment took me from the path to hell and placed me on my way to Heaven, and now in my heart dwells part of God, The Holy Ghost!

MY LORD

My Lord brings me joy, calmness and absolute peace

My Lord actually finds my feeble words of praise and my prayers to Him to be an honor, without cease

My Lord is the cause of all the good things in me, and in my life

My Lord is a shield against anger, confusion, greed and strife

My Lord loves and forgives me on a daily basis

My Lord keeps me humbled, so that I can grow and appreciate His blessings; in His hand, I'm held in the grip of His grace

My Lord always offers to guide my way

My Lord does this and much more! O, how I long to be with Him one glorious day!

I'M CLINGING TO MY LORD

This ole' world is always changing

But, with my Lord, I'm remaining

Folk all around me are giving in

But, with my Lord's help, I'll stride to be faithful to the end

The number of my persecutors may grow

But, in the end, the true intent of my heart will show

Nothing in this world will last
It will be worthless when this life here is passed
Everything will eventually slip through our fingers and be gone
All that will be left is our service for The Lord, and our eternal home
No matter what others may think or say
I'll cling to my Lord; with Him I'll stay

In good times, and in bad
I'm clinging to my Lord, just like He said
In victory and in the valleys
I'm clinging to my Lord and offering Him praise
On earth and some day in Heaven
I'm clinging to my Lord, for He purchased my freedom, my salvation

BIG MERCY

When God looked down upon wicked me
He had to show BIG mercy!
He showed me Jesus, crucified, and living again
Then He overshadowed me with conviction and caused me to repent of my sin!
The faith I needed, He supplied
Ever since then, I've been saved, now daily it is I who must die!
When God saved me
He had to change me, his heart was full of BIG mercy!
His power changes who I am daily, and causes me to grow
If it weren't for His BIG mercy, where I'd be now I do not know!
One great and happy day, Home Sweet Home I'll be
And, I'll bow before my Saviour and praise Him for His BIG mercy!

NEVER BEFORE

Never before had I felt such conviction
Until I saw myself through the eyes of The Holy Spirit of The Lord of all creation!

Never before had I felt the need to be born again
Until Jesus reached out to me those nail pierced hands!

Never before had I felt such peace and joy
Until Jesus washed all my sins away!

Never before had I cared about reading The Bible

Until Jesus saved me and said, "Read my Word, and follow..."

Never before had I been thrilled at the thought of eternity
Until Jesus saved me!

Never before had I cared about sharing the gospel
Until Jesus burdened me over lost souls!

Never before had I cared about praising His Name to others
Until I realized that He really is a Friend that sticketh closer than a brother!

Never before had I dared toss aside my own hopes, dreams or deepest wishes
Until He showed me that I am completely His!

Never before had I felt so humiliated or unworthy
Until I heard how Jesus bore my sins and died and arose for even me!

Never before have my lips desired to sing someone praise
Until Jesus put a song in my heart, to sing to Him throughout all my nights and days!

Never before have I longed to go somewhere I've never been to
Until Jesus said, "I have a mansion I've prepared just for you!"

AT LEAST ONE MIRACLE

PSALMS 13:5-6

Brethren, when we were saved, we saw the Miraculous Lord do a mighty work in our hearts
He saved my soul, I've seen at least one of His miracles; He gave me a brand new start
Yes, it is a miracle that I got saved
And it is yet another miracle, the way I since behave
Reading my Bible, it comes alive and speaks to me
It is a miracle that I now understand it, when once I just couldn't "see"
The forgiveness He has put in my heart for those who've hurt me in the past
Is yet another miracle, His forgiveness lasts
The things I once took pleasure or enjoyment in
They aren't the same to me, it's a miracle that I now see them as sin
My world has changed totally
And, it all stems back to the first miracle, the one that took place inside of me
All Christians should be aware of having witnessed at least one miracle
And, we ought to tell about it, in doing so, we may snatch others away from the devil
Praise The Lord for the miracle of true salvation!
Praise Him for giving our lives a new and solid Foundation!

LORD, YOU'VE CHANGED ME

Lord, I was a dirty sinner
Until You turned me into a "repentor"

Lord, I was a shameful "repentor"
Until You cleansed me and reassured me that, with You, I'm not a failure

Lord, I was a weak, helpless person at my best
Until You taught me how to daily crucify my flesh

Lord, You've given me a new life to live
Therefore, all I am and all I have to You, I give

Lord, You didn't owe me a thing
But, You sought me, bought me, and taught me the truth about Calvarys' salvation

And, You promise to carry me from death unto eternal life
All this, for repenting and believing in Jesus-leaving with You my worry and strife

Although it doesn't seem fair
I am thankful that You care

Lord, You've changed me
And given me the knowledge that I'll live a bright eternity!

MARCHING BAND

When I met my sweet Jesus, I cried because I was so happy!
He picked me up, brushed me off and gave me a uniform to wear, called "Christianity"
The Holy Spirit immediately moved inside of me, and with the instrument of my conscience,
    started playing simple tunes
He got my attention, and, I couldn't help but hear His orchestra inside telling me what to do
As I flipped through my "Hymnal for life", my Bible, my feet began to march in place
And, as I read the words, I came to understand their message of "forward march", as I desired
    to one day see The Lamb's face
I began marching, and right away, that creepy devil tried to coax me to march to his tune
But, I ignored him, because I knew what he was up to!
I've been marching ever since I was given the command that day
And, I trust in Jesus' commands, and intend to march to them as long as the marching band plays
And one day, when I'm ordered to be halted:
I will look to the sky, and prepare to be exalted!

HAVE I GOT JOY

1PETER 1:8-9

The Name of Jesus touches the depths of my soul
And, when 1 recall what He did for me, my joy begins to overflow!

The Words in my Bible tug at my heart-strings
And, when I obey their convictions, I'm filled with joy, because from it I receive blessings!

The thought of walking on the streets in Heaven overwhelms me
And fills me up with so much joy, that others can't help but see!

When I see others, who are His children, too, who sulk and walk, looking down
I just feel like saying, "My brother, since you know Jesus, turn that frown upside down!

HEAVEN ON MY MIND

I am saved, born again
I am now a real Christian
I am a pilgrim passing through this place
I am seeking and awaiting each day to see sweet Jesus' face
There is no place of refuge upon this earth for me
My Refuge is in my Saviour, I'm so glad He's with me on this journey
How my soul longs to be with my Lord and Saviour
How I long to meet Him Who saved me and changed my thoughts and behavior
I long to step upon the shore of my eternal home
How I long for the stress of this life to be gone
The things I enjoy the most here
I'm sure won't compare to what'll be over There!
In the midst of what I'm doing, I often leave it all behind
Because I've got Heaven on my mind!

I COULDN'T HELP IT

I couldn't help but be a sinner
And Lord, You loved me so much that you offered to be my Saviour
I couldn't help but live under the reins of evilness
You, Lord, humbled me to a point of true repentance
I couldn't help myself to stop living to follow my fleshly desires

Lord, Your Spirit shows me to desire a treasure that's "higher"

I couldn't help but submit my all when on my heart God's Spirit did call

You Lord, saved me by grace when I used the gift You gave me, of faith

Lord, I couldn't help what I was, before You

Thank You for daily molding me to be a creature that's made anew

Lord, I can't help but yearn to live with You one day, in Glory

My lips long to praise You, with the choir of saints, and sing, "For Thou Art Worthy!"

UNTIL JESUS CAME

I was bound to spend eternity in hell, the flames were so eager to consume me

The fiery flames were about to burn me, until Jesus came in the form of a "Fireman" and saved me from the burning building, and set me free

I was bound to drown in the sea of my sins

Until Jesus came to me in the form of a "Lifeguard", and pulled me out, rinsed me in His blood, and left me free and cleansed

I was about to choke on this world's pollution

Until Jesus came to me in the form of a "Physician", and hooked me up to an everlasting supply of fresh oxygen

I was wallowing in my tears of loneliness

Until Jesus came to me in the form of a "Friend" and gave me the assurance of togetherness

I was about to take a permanent tour through the lake of fire and brimstone

When Jesus came to me in the form of a "Tour Guide" and is leading me to my Heavenly Home

I was about to be towed to hell, when I broke down

Until Jesus came to me in the form of a "Tow Truck" and started towing me in the opposite direction, heading to a glorious Town

I was burning with the earthly desire to be greater

Until Jesus came and quenched it, in the form of a wonderful Lord and Saviour!

LORD, LET ME

Lord, when I look down

Let me be reminded by The Holy Spirit that You're all around!

Lord, in my times of happiness

Let me remember that it's all because of Your blessings!

Lord, when I steer wrong

Let mw be guided by You, to be back where I belong!

Lord, when I'm in my moments of "glory"

Let me be humbled, because it's all due to Your grace and glory!

Lord, when I begin juggling my own problems

Let me realize that I must depend upon You to take over and solve them!

Lord, whatever good things I make happen in my life

Let me reflect on the fact that You have been my Guide!

Lord, when I enter into Heaven someday

Let me quickly be on bended knee before Jesus, to thank Him for "paving the way!"

Chapter Five

Pathway From Bitterness

Let all bitterness, and wrath, and anger, and clamour, and
evil speaking, be put away from you, with all malice: And
be ye kind one to another, tenderhearted, forgiving one
another, even as God for Christ's sake hath forgiven you.

Ephesians 4:31-32

GIVE JESUS YOUR BEST

Dearest brothers and sisters in Christ, our Saviour
Let's be challenged to offer to Jesus our greatest behavior
Give Jesus your best service
One great day, it will be worth it
Give Him your best attention
This is sins best prevention
Let's offer up fervent prayers, from the depths of our hearts
And wait to see what this starts
Witness to others with a true concern
And perhaps they'll accept Jesus, and will never burn
Sing unto Jesus songs of praise
And He will bless us with joyful days
Keep a clean temple for the Holy Spirit, your permanent Guest
Remember to keep all your sins confessed
Seek to empty of self and become full of His Spirit
Obey His Still, Small Voice, when you hear it
It is possible to give Jesus your best
For, we abide in Him and obey Him, and He does the rest
His strength and grace truly are sufficient
Let's give our best to Jesus, and be humble, and diligent
If we do it from our heart, as led by His Spirit, it will be counted, we'll be called faithful
Keep it up, and when He appears, we won't be shameful

I AM NOT MY OWN

Each day, my Lord asks me some questions
And He gives me more guidance and convictions
God told me that I need to examine self
He tells me to answer to Him, not to everyone else
Upon salvation, The Spirit of Jesus moved in
He knows my every good deed as well as my every sin
What does He catch me thinking about?
Does He see evil thoughts, unbelief or doubt?
Does He see lovely, pure thoughts of goodness?
Whatever He reveals, I must show true repentance
What does He hear my tongue speak of?
Does He hear me glorifying Him, above?
Does He hear evil words, gossip or chaos?
Does He constantly hear me grumble, complain and fuss?
What does Jesus see my hands doing?
Does He see them working and serving?
Does He find them lazy, being idle and slack?
Does He find them giving, or giving and then taking right back?
What does He see my eyes gazing upon?
Does He see them reading His Word, or a poem or song?
Does He see them looking to Him in prayer?
Does He see them stray; or cut others down with no compassion, not a care?
Where does He notice my feet traveling to?
Does He see them being faithful and true?
Does He see them going here and there to share the gospel with another?
Does He see them rush to help a needy sister or brother?

EXAMINE YOURSELF

Since I have a Saviour Named Jesus
I have accepted Him as the propitiation for my sins
I try to be a devoted Christian
I try to witness about what He's done for me
In doing this, God still tells me to daily examine myself
How??

Trying to live as sin-free as possible, and repent to Jesus, seeking His forgiveness when The
  Holy Spirit shows me that I slipped up

Since I have Jesus in your heart, I yearn to be as close as possible to His behavior, attitude, likes
  and dislikes

When? All of the time

I really want to be a witness to others, that I am a part of Christ, examine myself, and stride to
  do what's right!

COMPARISONS FOR SIN

Think of sin as a hungry shark, lurking around
Waiting to attack and swallow a piece of us down
Think of sin as deep, choking quicksand
Waiting to swallow us, when in it, we step or stand
Think of sin as a hissing snake, with venomous fangs drooling with poison
Waiting to strike and weaken us, when we give in to temptation
Think of sin as satan's opened palms, reaching to grasp yours
Waiting to pull you to him, when Jesus convicts and you refuse to listen any more
Think of sin as Lucifer's nickname
Waiting to be called on by us, to bring us destruction and shame
Think of sin as a phone call to our soul, internally ringing
Waiting for us to answer and begin suffering
Think of sin as a tornado sweeping through a beautiful valley
Waiting to suck you in, as Jesus pleads with your heart, "Please don't turn your back on me!"
Think of sin as throwing mud on Jesus' Name
Telling God that Name isn't precious, for a few moments of time
Think of sin as shooting arrows, piercing into God's heart
Imagine the pain He feels when the shooting starts
Think of sin as tears from Heaven
Waiting to stop when you stop sinning and start repenting!

IT'S WORTH IT TO ME

God says it
And, we should find worth in it
Filling up on His Word each day
We should live in a new way...

It's worth it to me to avoid getting angry

It's worth it to me to be forgiving to my enemies

It's worth it to me to make a daily sacrifice of my flesh

It's worth it to me to seek to live humbly, and try to obey The Holy Spirit and my conscience

It's worth it to me to let all life's worries roll on by me

It's worth it to me to put all my faith in The One ruling the Sweet By and By!

It's worth it to me to tell everyone I know

About Jesus, Who will one great day bring me to my REAL HOME!

It's all worth it to me, because I know it's pleasing to Him

It's worth it all, to me, because it blesses my heart when I seek to obey Him

SATAN'S GOAL

Let me tell you about satan's goal

He tempts us to sin, and when we do, he laughs as we face trouble

He gives us negative and confusing thoughts

He will do anything in an attempt to tear us apart from God

He can cause our conscience to be reluctant, and tries to fog up our mind

Number one on his list is for us to leave the Word of God behind

He tempts us with lust, prestige, riches and pleasure

And tries to keep us from repenting, in desperation to keep us from discovering God's treasure

Satan wants us to doubt God and ignore the conviction The Holy Ghost speaks within us

Satan tries to build disbelief and cause us to be skeptical about the blessings laid before us,
     from Jesus

Satan will try to take away every little thing that is dear to our heart

If we allow him even a crack in our lives, he will try to seep in and tear it apart!

ARE THERE GOOD SINS?

If you find yourself trying to justify your sins

Know that the devil is trying to get you to justify it, so that you'll do it again and again

If you sin, and do not repent or feel as though you've let Jesus down

You are treading on dangerous ground

Satan's goal is to tempt you to sin a little more and a little more

In hopes that you'll lose touch with your conscience and your Saviour

Instead of justifying your sins, turn to Jesus and ask for help in realizing that it is wrong

And, in doing this over and over, you get spiritual exercise and begin to be spiritually strong

PLEASING TO JESUS

When I got saved, I wept for joy, that The Holy Ghost touched me!

I gave thanks and praise, that He convicted me enough to get me on bended knees!

Jesus met me there, and I invited Him into my temple to dwell

In there, His light is always burning to show me the path that our Father spelled

Since I am the one who invited Him in, I consider Him to be my guest

Therefore; I stride to obey Him, and behave my best!

Before I speak, before I dwell on a thought, before I react, before I make any choices

I stride to confer first with The Holy Ghost dwelling inside of me, and ask if my words,
    thoughts, reactions and choices are pleasing to Jesus!

THE CONSTANT BATTLE

I am in the midst of a battle, every moment of time

It is a battle against principalities, which takes place around me, and even in my mind

Satan is always relentlessly attacking

Just as I escape one fiery dart, more are on the way, to begin their stalking

On my own, I couldn't last a second against the enemy

I can only defeat him through the strength of Jesus, Who dwells inside of me

Satan can cause injuries to me, especially if I'm not wearing the full armour of God

Therefore, I will hold up the shield of faith

This will protect me day after day

I will carry the Sword of the spirit, and wear the helmet of salvation

I will put on daily the breastplate of righteousness, and my feet shod with the gospel of peace,
    in preparation

And, I will speak boldly and pray and wrestle against spiritual wickedness

I must prepare over and over for the constant battle described in the sixth chapter of Ephesians

BLACK CLOUDS

Christian, think of each sin you commit as being a black cloud hanging over your life

If you do not repent and become cleansed from them, they will continue adding up blocking
    out more and more of God's light, causing you darkness and strife

You do not need to have gloomy days, when you have the right to have sunny ones

Do like first John says, and confess your sins, and then watch the black clouds dissolve and be
    replaced with the warm rays of "The Son"

Don't wait to be so bogged down by black clouds that a storm forms and the thunder begins to
    rumble
When God sees that storm swirling about, He waits to see what you will do-stay stubborn, or
    become humble
If He sees you stubbornly ignoring the storm, for your own good, He allows it to continue,
    and , the discipline begins
God allows these storms because He loves you and wants you humbled within
Just remember that a clear conscience is like a clear day
And, when the black clouds start appearing, they eventually form something: a stormy day!

SPIRITUAL POVERTY

I believe that faith in The Lord brings blessings in return
A while back, I felt as though I was lacking faith and became concerned
I found myself in spiritual poverty, in other words, in great need for faith, to gain more
So, I gave more time to my Lord, and He added to my spiritual wealth, and left me not as
    destitute, as poor
And, the more I received from being close to Him, the better I felt; therefore, I craved more
    and more
I realized that He constantly quenches that craving, after creating a new thirst in me, leaving
    me fuller each time, than before
I may not have worldly wealth, I seem to this world to be insignificant
But, I have great wealth that I treasure deep inside that is very significant, because it's Heaven sent!

EACH TIME

Christians, each time we find ourselves in sin
We must realize that we've turned our face from The Lord, and disobeyed Him
Each time we give in to temptation and sin
We must realize that there's a crack in our life, allowing satan in
Each time we commit even an ignorant sin
We must know that our conscience won't sit quite right, because of The Holy Ghost, living within
Each time we turn our back on The Lord, and sin
We must repent and truly seek to be forgiven
Each time we know something's wrong, and do it anyway, it's still called sin
We must recognize that we should have followed The Lord's conviction at the beginning
Each time we realize we've committed sin

We must admit it to The Lord, and ask Him to help us learn a valuable lesson
Each time we have been forgiven for a sin
We should give thanks and praise to God for allowing us the privilege us using Jesus' blood for our sin offering

FINGERPRINTS

Every word we say and deed we do leave something behind: our fingerprints
Whether we speak and act pleasing or not, our prints leave behind our resemblance
If our fingerprints exist on something called sin
We need to come to the Throne of God and ask to be forgiven
Although His shed blood erases our fingerprints from His remembrance
We will still be faced with the consequence
From His memory, our fingerprints will be blotted away
But, that doesn't mean that we will be immune to that sins repercussions, when they come to haunt us some day
And, when people uncover our fingerprints, on good and bad things
We should either give glory to God, or ask others toward us to be forgiving
Remember that The Lord sees the fingerprints that we don't call on Him to erase
Therefore, we should stride with His help, to leave fingerprints in good places, and if not, we should immediately fall on our knees before The Throne of Grace!

THE DIVINE EXAMPLE

There was One Who came, lived sin free, died and arose again, for the sake of our salvation
And, I believe that just accepting our salvation from Him isn't enough
After being saved, we should, by His Spirit, try to follow the examples He lay before us
There is only One, that is The Divine Example for us to look up to
Only Jesus is sin free, but know that He yearns for us to try to follow and be true
He is so merciful, He grants us forgiveness when we sin and repent, all because He loves us supremely and eternally
Praise God that Jesus, The Divine Example, guides us, loves and forgives us, unconditionally!

HOW TO CRUCIFY YOUR FLESH

First of all, you must realize that it's not your own

Christian, you are simply a vessel, a means for The Word of God to spread, to flow

If you feel that you are in ownership of your own self

I suggest that you repeatedly let the verses from first Corinthians six nineteen and twenty flow
   from your mouth

Once you realize that you are not your own

It's easier to submit yourself to your owner, and then you're more eager to reap what you sow

You will come to a point in which you accept the realization

That you are not for yourself to control, you are God's creation

After this, when the news isn't so fresh

You will look back and see that you are carrying a cross, in which to attach the lusts of your flesh

Anything that The Holy Spirit disapproves of, speaking to you inside

You should try quickly to attach it to that cross dragging behind you, to hang and die

JUST A LITTLE BIT WON'T HURT

Imagine seeing someone with lung cancer

Picture someone saying to them, "want a smoke?"

And, they say, "sure, just a little bit won't hurt"

Imagine seeing someone make a donation, in hopes of helping to stop drunk driving

Picture someone holding out a beer, saying, "want a drink?"

And, they say, "sure, just a little bit won't hurt"

Imagine seeing a Christian

Picture satan bringing them a temptation, saying, "do you want some, it's special, from me?"

And they say, "sure, just a little bit won't hurt"

A little bit of sin will lead to a bad testimony, disaster or addiction

So, of course even a little bit of sin can affect a Christian

YOUR CONSCIENCE HAS QUESTIONS

Believers in Christ are Christians

When we become a Christian, immediately The Holy Spirit flows through us, with convictions

I have felt, many times, The Holy Spirit present my conscience with questions

He questions, convicts and offers to guide me, but I do the actions

Something I've learned is that the devil works over-time on us, especially after we've met Jesus

That devil will stop at nothing to deceive us; one of his missions is to muffle our conscience, trying to cause the truth of God's Word to leave us

Why does he try to muffle our conscience? you may ask

Because it asks us questions, like, "would Jesus want you to think, act or speak like this? Does this glorify God? Is it worth the temporary pleasure to give in to this temptation, and in it bask?"

Pray to Jesus for the victory

Ask Him to help you to be the best Christian you can be!

FAITH

EPHESIANS 6:16

If we have faith that Jesus was, is and always will be

If we have faith that He is the propitiation for our sins, that only He can make us righteous, for the eyes of God to see

If faith can bring us to trust in these facts

Then, through faith our sorrow, anger, bitterness, confusion, loneliness, hopelessness and strife can be laid to rest

If we have faith that He is the Powerful, Almighty, mountain-moving, sea-splitting, dead-raising, Redeeming, Sovereign, Soon Coming King and Lord

Then, surely, we can look to Him to lift away our fears, insecurities, impatience, bitterness, anger and so much more

And, faith keeps us believing that not only will He take these from us, but He will pour out peace, hope and love upon us and through us

And, we soon learn to have faith when our adversary shoots fiery darts at us, that they'll not be able to go through our shield of faith, which protects us

I SEE TEMPLES

Since The Lord has helped me grow in Him, to go to another level

I just cannot look at things the same

I have invited Jesus in, to run my temple, a job too big for me

I try to always ask Him to guide my decisions; and He convicts me to try to stop living to satisfy my flesh

I gave up so many little things, I was unaware of, that were offending Him, living within

I try to forsake anger and worry, I try to forsake finding pleasure in worldly things, and stocking up on this worlds' goods

And, each time, with His help, I make another little sacrifice, I see something new, from Him,
  of which I'm blessed!

Sometimes, when I look at others, through His eyes, I see temples

I see people smoking, cursing, despising others, and living in worry and stress; I pray for them,
  and thank God it isn't me, and for His daily convictions, trying to keep my spirit humble

I know I cannot live a perfect life, but with Jesus, I'll at least try

And, I just couldn't try to live right, if my temple was without Jesus to be my Guide

THIS IS HOW MY BOSS WORKS

Can you imagine making an error on your job, and being eager to tell your boss you've done wrong?

Can you imagine your boss guaranteeing to erase your mistake from existence, and telling you
  that on file your mistake doesn't belong?

What if your boss told you that because you learned your lesson you'd receive a raise?

Would you not leave your boss in wonderment and feeling a bit dazed?

Could you imagine going back to work and making another mistake, having to admit that
  once again, you've erred?

What if your boss said, "I can clearly see that you realize the error of your way, it'll be
  forgotten, you won't be fired!" ?

Would you not walk away, again, surprised, but feel as though you were an important asset?

You would say to yourself, "My boss sure is forgiving and compassionate!"

How nice to know for sure, that you have room to grow and learn, without ever losing your
  position!

How good it is to repent of your mistakes and know for sure that you'll be forgiven!

How exciting, when you picture yourself in the future

To know that you have the freedom to learn from your mistakes (which develops character)

No, I'm not in fantasy land...

This is how my Boss, Jesus, works, He told me so the moment I grasped His hand!

GOLD PLATED HEART

EZEKIEL 36:26-27

Before my heart was cleansed by the Righteous blood of Jesus, I just had an ordinary heart

And, that heart showed others sympathy and compassion, that I thought carried far

But, after my heart was cleansed in Jesus' blood, I felt such an enormous change start

Now, it's as though I have a gold plated heart

And, this new heart can unconditionally forgive, and even tries to be forgetful

This new heart tries to show brotherly love
And, this new heart is burdened to share with others the news about an eternal Home, above
Yes, my heart was cleansed by the blood of the King of Kings
And, it became "gold plated", and changed my everything!

CONVICTED

The turbulence that was stirring about in my soul
Has faded, because The Lord showed me the way to self control
My heart has been convicted to do what's right
And, I will stride to obey, with all my might
With Jesus, I can face lucifer, himself
And tell him, in Jesus' Name, to go some place else
For, in me, there's no room for him to dwell
All the temptations that will come my way
I will try, with God's help, to turn them away
My feet were slippery beneath me
Until The Lord, through forgiveness, wiped them clean
And gave me, yet, another chance
To be strong in His strength, and overcome temptation; and, in His strength, to take a stronger
    stance
And to confess my sins, showing true repentance
This does not mean that I'll never sin again
I'm going to sin, because I'm human
But, I sure am grateful for the forgiveness He made available to us
Through the free gift of salvation through Lord Jesus, Who suffered, Who was our sacrifice
    upon that old, rugged cross

AT MY OWN FUNERAL

I was brought low, and finally accepted Jesus Christ as my personal Saviour, as many others
    have done
So, to those not belonging to Him, I seem like just "another one"
Something very real happened, and I am compelled to share it with anyone willing to listen
Trusting Jesus as Saviour is much more than words, or a "profession"
When His Spirit wanted to live inside, I invited, "welcome"
I repented, due to an overwhelming conviction

I tried to be good, thirsting to read His Word

It became obvious to me, one evening, as I was reading my Bible, and stopping to pray

I was shown that I don't belong to myself, but to Him, and I learned that I must die to self each day

He showed me some verses that tugged on the reins of my heart

And, The Holy Ghost said, "The funeral must start"

I submitted my mind, words, feelings, my whole being and all of my earthly possessions

I imagined seeing myself laying in death, and like Jesus, resurrecting

The old me has been dying ever since, and when I now look in the mirror I seek to see not mine, but Jesus face

When I speak, I desire to use the words that He would have me to say; I stride to not cause my Father look upon me as a disgrace

When I think, I ask Jesus to guide my thoughts

After all, those, too, His blood bought

When I dress for the day, I ask Him if it's appropriate

And, when He says no, I try not to argue, but to try to be obedient

I will never be, do, think or say all that The Lord would have me to

But, at the same time, I choose, daily, to try to be diligent, on the job, and I seek to never be labeled as "lazy" or "untrue"

Jesus suffered, died and rose because He was dedicated to His cause

And, because of what He did for me, I stride to please Him, even though that means I must daily pick up and carry my own cross

CHRISTIAN IN TRAINING

When we accept God's gift of salvation, our Christian journey begins immediately

Although we submitted to Jesus everything we have, we still need training for our Christian journey

Even though we have become a new creature

We must still train on how to behave "pure"

We must train on how to step out of our old thinking patterns

And, we need to be trained on how to put on the armour of God, that's mentioned in The Bible, in one of Paul's letters of truth, guidance and concerns

Every job requires a training period in which we learn the do's and don'ts

And, it is the job of every Christian to read and study God's words and commandments

Each of us will be a Christian in training

Until we find ourselves glorified, and in Heaven, singing and praising

We must never be lazy about learning and serving

Because we are expected to minister to this world, that is always growing

THE ROOT OF BITTERNESS

HEBREWS 12:1, 15
EPHESIANS 4:22-32, 5:8-10, 17, 6:6-7
ROMANS 12:18

God warns us in His Word not to be deceived

We can identify wrong spirits and doctrine

But, do we identify what we may have growing, within?

We wouldn't go to certain "churches", because God says it's wrong

We wouldn't fellowship with satan, because with him, we don't belong

We hold up our shield of faith, when our enemy shoots

But, do we realize what could be growing in us, taking deep root?

Ask God to shed light, exposing you, within

If you see bitterness, call it what it is, call it SIN

The more you nurture it, the stronger it will become

If you've been ignoring it, you're letting it win

Ask God to help you dig deep and uproot it

Before it controls your life, and takes your testimony, to ruin it

Take heed not to hold on to your bitterness

Take heed not to disobey The Lord's convictions

Choosing to let bitterness keep it's root within

Is also choosing to be the recipient of God's chastening

Don't you see that keeping bitterness in your heart hurts your own self

It keeps you from receiving God's best, and from spiritual "good health"

Bitterness quenches The Spirit and hurts the heart of The Lord

Be thou encouraged to hold on to it no more!

How can we fully serve God and ask Him to bless us

When we allow what satan planted to grow in us?

LORD, PLEASE SMOTHER ME

Lord, I wish to be smothered by Your holiness and grace
And, I, in return will smother You in thanks and praise

Lord, smother me with Your protection
And I will smother my "enemies" with kindness and affection

Dear Lord, smother me with Your wisdom
And I will tell everyone I can about salvation and Your Kingdom

God, please smother me with Your forgiveness
And I will show you repentance

Jesus, please smother me with thoughts of You dying on that cruel cross
So that when I come to a river of evil, I can easily make it across

I CAN HEAR, BUT NOT BE HEARD

PSALM 66:18 & 1JOHN 1:9

Since God saved my soul and moved into my heart
His Still, Small Voice, from me, will not depart
No matter if I'm doing wrong or right, He speaks to me
Whether I'm far away, or by His side, His voice is heard clearly
When I read my Bible, and when I pray, I hear Him speak
His Still, Small Voice talks to me when my faith's strong, and even when it's weak
No matter what I do, and where I go, He has something to say
When I lose direction, He tells me the way

Now, on the other hand, I must pay special attention that I'm heard
For, if I stray from God, He'll not hear a word
If I hold on to a known sin, not confessing and trying to forsake it
I can pray all day and night, and He won't listen a bit
Just like a parent rewards their child for being good
So does my Heavenly Father hear and answer my prayers when I try to obey as I should

So, it is possible that I can hear, but not be heard
Lord, help me keep my sin accounts short, so You can listen to my every word
Father, help me to stay by Your side
So that You will hear when in You I confide

Chapter Six

Pathway From Idleness

See then that ye walk circumspectly, not as fools, but as wise,
Redeeming the time, because the days are evil. Romans 5:15-16

JUST ONE DAY

Brethren, what would happen if we decided to deny Christ for just one day?

What if we toss His Word aside, and forsake morning, noon and evening prayer?

What if we denied our tongue the chance of testifying of Him?

What if, for just one day, our praising Him found an end?

What if, for just one day, we forbid our hands to pass out tracts?

What if, for just one day, we choose not to examine ourselves and realize our slackness?

Just one day like this can make us cold and bitter...

Day after day like this, and in our hearts it feels like winter!

What if, this day, we turn to Him and repent?

What if we acknowledge the fact that we are not our own, we belong fully to Him?

Let TODAY be the day of repentance...

And this will surely be a day of forgiveness and of being a true Christian witness!

I CHOOSE CHRIST'S STRENGTH

PSALMS 84:10

In the daily battle for my Lord

I must prepare just as I did the day before

I must put on the armour of God

And seek wisdom and strength from Him, above

My strength will end in my defeat

However, if I battle by Christ's strength, victory is guaranteed!

How can my "sword" do any good

When I do not read it and hide it in my heart as I should?

Lord, I commit all of me toward Your work in this world, beneath

And, I choose to go forward in Your strength!

CHRISTIANS, WHERE ARE YOU?

Needy souls can be found everywhere

Christians, where are you? Are you making a difference there?

Discouraged brethren are hindered and in despair

Christians, where are you? Are you showing that you care?

Diseased, lame and sick persons are desiring that your time you would share

Christians, where are you? Won't you take a moment to pay them a visit and lift up a prayer?

The Pastor is waiting for prayer meetings to begin, wondering who will dare

Christians, where are you? Do you not want to speak with Jesus, your Mediator?

Jesus is watching how we spend our time; He has counted our every hair

Christians, where are you? Don't you realize that He's everywhere?

IF YOU KNEW

If you knew you'd be blind in the morning, then would you spend time reading Gods' Word this night?

If you knew you'd be deaf in one week, then would you go to all the church services to hear good preaching?

If you knew you'd never be able to speak again, starting in one day, then would you pray for and try to tell others about Jesus?

If you knew that you only had six months to live, then would you give quality time to your family, and service to your Lord?

If you knew this day what the next day would bring, you might do more witnessing, praising and praying!

But, we don't know if we'll be allowed another day, so why not live like today is our last day?

THE LOST IN YOUR LIFE

What if???

Their salvation was hinged on YOUR prayers, alone...

What if???

Someone told you that before YOU were saved they shed tears and entreated God, on YOUR behalf...

What if???

The people you pray for, so heartlessly, go to hell, and you hear their wailing, screaming and cursing, and you see their gnashing teeth and the smoke of their torment!

Then, would you be burdened???

When it's too late?

What good will it do to finally listen to The Holy Spirit, when it's too late, that person dies, or the rapture occurs?

Good intentions do not get results!

Vain prayers do not get results!

Doubting while praying does not get results!

Get a hold of the Throne of God! Beg Him! Stand in the gap!

If the burden for their souls is not there, be concerned, and pray to have a burden for them!

Listen...

The clock is ticking!

Look...

The Lord will be back at any moment!

Get busy praying and witnessing...

Now!

Later is TOO LATE!

THE CHOICE IS YOURS

So many Christians cry out that they want revival to break out one day

They may even ask God to send it, when they pray

Many Christians get stirred and thirsty, but change not and remain dry

And then when revival doesn't come, they wonder why

They ask why God hasn't sent "fire" from Heaven

As they keep their eyes on everyone else's sins

So many Christians want the prize, but won't pay the price

They'll keep saying they want revival, when in their hearts, they're not willing to sacrifice

They want to see revival, but deep down inside, they don't want it to start with self

So, they wait and pray, hoping to see it in someone else

They thirst for the entertainment they think it will bring

But, when and if it comes, they haven't contributed anything

So many Christians are full of this world and self

That, though they pray for it, they leave revival on a shelf

Dear Christian friend, what do you choose to do?

Do you want to see it in others, or let it begin with you?

FREE THE SLAVES

The only freedom satan gives to his roaming souls

Is the chance to sin more, and dig themselves into deeper holes

He wants to tempt them enough to sin a little more here and there

And, when they give in, he overtakes more of them, by placing his temptations, disguised, everywhere

He encourages their freedom

To ignore Jesus, their only chance of escaping eternal damnation

He loves getting souls caught up in a vicious cycle

Of feeling sad, worried, selfish and confused enough to seek a quick pleasure, and sin, and continue being anything but humble

So many people are slaves for him, without even realizing it

He causes people to complain about various things to anyone who will listen

And, this causes an atmosphere which actually glorifies the problem, therefore, glorifying him

He loves people to gossip about one another, to become envious, insecure and jealous

Which, subconsciously, causes them, toward him, to be zealous

Which, in turn, keeps them under the crack of his whip

Which is sure to be a one way, hell-bound trip

The only power that can overcome him, and free his slaves

Is for Christians to bring The Word of God to them, through The Holy Spirit, before they die, because then it'll be too late

We have all been a slave to him in one way or another

But, it's up to the ones who have been freed to pass on God's Word, which is the only way to save others!

IF YOU REALLY KNOW JESUS

PROVERBS 15:9 & ROMANS 10:11

You say that you have a "pal" that hung on a cross and rose to give forgiveness

First, you must realize that He's not a "pal", He's the Powerful, Miraculous, Humbling, Almighty Saviour, Jesus!

If you really know Jesus, you can be filled with joy and peace in the midst of trials and tragedy!

If you really know Jesus, your lips can deliver words of comfort and love in the midst of sadness and confrontation!

If you really know Jesus, you can rejoice at His strength to help you pass by temptations without giving them much thought!

If you really know Jesus, you can be thankful for the simplest things in your life, instead of looking to see what else can be attained or bought!

If you really know Jesus, your mind can rebuke negative, vengeful thoughts, and loving and forgiving others can be something you do!

If you really know Jesus, you can be anew, because of the changes The Holy Spirit makes in you!

If you really know Jesus, you can share the exciting news about what He's done!

If you really know Jesus, you should be convicted by your own sin, and cringe when around others that do, because of Godly wisdom!

If you really know Jesus, you can stride to live according to the example He set!

If you really know Jesus, you can pick up your own cross, daily, and crucify your flesh!

Those who know Jesus Christ are not supposed to be trying to figure out on their own life's purpose and meaning

They ought to be in His Word, seeking His will, and gaining understanding!

Those who really know Jesus can turn from worldly pleasures, treasures, loves and lusts; and look, instead, daily to the One Who gave of self to us, upon Calvary's cross!

Those who really know Jesus can experience the power of prayer as they feebly talk into the ears of The Lord, Who will hear!

I DESIRE TO BE FOUND GUILTY

2CORINTHIANS 5:20a

Since I've been bought by the blood of The Lamb

I am a daughter of The Great I AM!

He is my Daddy, and He takes extra good care of me

There are always clothes on my back, a roof over my head, and food in my tummy!

My Father gave me some rules to follow, and He makes Himself clear as to what pleases Him

And, He promised that soon He is coming back, again!

When death calls me Home, or if first, He comes back, and His precious face I finally see

I desire to be found "guilty" of pleasing Him, praising Him or praying to Him to help me be the best Ambassador for Him that I can be!

IMPOSTER CHRISTIANS

Some people say they're Christian, and even act like one on Sundays

But, if you bump into them any other day, you can't help but be concerned and pray

Study what the meaning of Christian is and you'll see that they are meant to resemble The Christ, Jesus

And, they do it because they desire to, not because they "must"

It takes faith in Jesus, and Holy Spirit conviction

To become a real born again Christian

It is impossible to be a Christian, and at the same time, see nothing wrong with sin

Yes, Christians are not perfect, but they stride, in Jesus' strength to avoid sinning, and when they do, their heart condemns their actions, convicting them that they ought to repent and try not to do it again

As a born again Christian, with God's Spirit indwelling me, it breaks my heart to see an imposter, a pretender, a phony, a fake

They do not bring any glory to God's Name, but cause others, of His Word, to forsake

How sad, that some of these imposters seem to think that they are pulling the wool over other's eyes

But, they can be seen for what they really are by The Saviour, no matter their disguise

Christians ought not judge or gossip about them

But, rather pray that they'll come to the realization

That being a Christian is not acting, but believing that Hebrews four twelve is true

And, if the imposter could only realize this, they'd be able to look in the mirror, saying, "you're deceiving only you"

Christians shouldn't feel as though they have something to hide

They should be willing to open their heart on any given day, inviting skeptics to look inside

Their lives should be a reflection

Of their Lord's saving of them, and of a daily connection

Christians know that the imposter is not completely to blame

He chose to be weak when the deceiving devil came

Imposter Christians need not be ignored

They are lost souls that must be won to The Lord!

WHEN YOU'RE SERIOUS

If you take The Lord serious, shouldn't you act like you do?

If you are always silly or sarcastic when "witnessing" for Him, how will others believe you know the truth?

If you are God's child

You ought to have changes in your life, that aren't only mild

When you meet Jesus and accept Him as your Saviour

You can't help but change at least some of the ways you think, act, talk, and live; you'll have some new behavior

If The Lord answers your prayers

Let others know; tell them that if they turn to Him, He'll answer theirs

If you are serious about winning someone to The Lord

Don't laugh with them when they brag about the sins they committed just the day before

If you laugh, too, you're giving the wrong impression

If you take even a little part in it, or seem to approve, or act comfortable around it

They will not get the message you might of intended; how can they get the message when on it, you sit?

Be the example, the messenger, the "different" one

And then you're really trying to get your assignment done!

Chapter Seven

Pathway of Service

Be ye strong therefore, and let not your hands be weak: for
your work shall be rewarded.   2Chronicles 15:7

SERVING GOD

How can we serve God, without serving others?
In order to serve Him, we must serve each other!
What joy it brings to our own lives...
When we share, care, encourage and pray for those in need or strife!
We serve God when we truly do unto others as we would want done unto ourselves!
Christians, let's serve others, above all else!

THE BUS KIDS

I'm so thankful to be a part of a church that brings kids in each Sunday on vans and buses
They are precious, even if they're not dressed up, and if they have dirty little faces
The gleam in their eyes as they pass by with a smile
Makes me glad they came, and assures me that all the time spent on them is worth while
Some come from broken, unloving homes
Some come sick as could be, some even come in a cast, with a broken bone
They come in good health and bad, when they're happy and when they're sad
I try to make them feel special, realizing that the love I offer may be all that they have
I hope I'm a good reflection of Jesus' love to them
That they may know that He loves them and wants them to obtain salvation
My heart's burden is that they understand the way to Heaven, and respect God and His Word
And, when they're driving out of sight, waving out the windows, I pray that they'll remember
   the Sunday School lessons they've learned
I hope that they accept Jesus, relying on Him for salvation
And, that they help their family members, friends and neighbors claim Heaven, too, as their
   destination!

DON'T BE AFRAID

MARK 16:15

Come to church for soul-winning and visitation time
Be part of the special group of Christians finding lost souls, and being kind
Don't be afraid to knock on a stranger's door
Don't be afraid to tell them about The Lord
Don't let fear keep you from obeying God's great commission
Go share the gospel with others, show God true submission!

ABIDE BY YOUR SIDE

So many things in this ever-changing world come and go
I stay bust so much, but have so little to show
In the midst of all that I cannot depend upon
Is The One Who keeps telling me to press on
It is You, Lord, Who is my Saviour and Guide
You speak truth to me, though the whole world may lie
The farther I am from You, the darker and louder the storms seem to be
But, as I draw nigh, I trade fear and restlessness for tranquility
As the world changes, You stay the same
Though the fruit doesn't show right away, You tell me to keep busy, trying to bring glory to
    Your Name
You remind me that whether I'm on mountaintops high or valleys deep and wide
That I must always stride to abide by Your side

THE CHRISTIAN BOOKSTORE

DEDICATED TO MY FRIENDS AT MY FAVORITE BOOK STORE

I remember years ago, my first time in the Christian bookstore
It was unlike any store I'd been in before
How friendly were the faces that met me
How amazing, that they really were godly!
I had been in a store or two through the years, but, they were liberal, and religious
But, this store not only promotes Him, but the employees walk with Jesus
Over the years, they have been there for my many needs
If they didn't have what I desired, they ordered it, showing ease
At times, I have come with a broken spirit

Oh, the words of encouragement they offered gave me a lift

And, when I came in with rejoicing in my heart

They, too, rejoiced, then the testifying began to start

I remember their many words of wisdom

I remember the owners' wife offering me a book on how to raise my sons

Each person there has offered words fitly spoken to me

And advice, encouragement, even praying when I shared with them a need

Oh, the many hours I have spent looking through all the godly books they offer

And the many that I purchased have thus far been worth every dollar

It's nice to have a place to go in this day and age

To shop for Bibles and Christian aids

All the lives that have been touched through the tracts they sell

And the lives changed by the written page, all the souls that have been saved from hell

I'm sure that The Lord is keeping track of where all the fruit stems from

And, I'm sure that they give all the thanks and praise to God's Son!

MY INHERITANCE

1PETER 4:10

If you receive a call one day...

And are told you have an inheritance to claim, wouldn't you long to have it, right away?

Suppose you claim it, and realize that it is a never ending supply

Wouldn't you be overcome with joy, deep inside?

Now, suppose you are told that each person in the world is offered the same inheritance to
    claim, as you did...

Wouldn't you feel obligated to mention such news to all those you come in contact with?

THE TIMER

Just as a pie sits, baking, in a timed oven...

We're on this earth, but, we do not know when Jesus will make His next coming...

Just as we can see when the pie is close to being done...

We should know that the season is nigh, soon the rapture will happen and, the tribulation will
    begin

The pie may be done, though, before the timer stops

The beginning of the end of this world may come sooner than we thought

The timer is always ticking...

Reminding the lost, to Jesus, to stop resisting
To Jesus, their hearts they should bring...
Because no one knows just when the timer will "ding"
Dear Christians, are you telling others...
That there's not much time?...tell strangers, neighbors, parents, cousins, sisters and brothers...

WHAT IF

What if you noticed that I could of saved someone from stepping out in front of oncoming traffic, but I didn't...
Instead, I just looked away!

What if you noticed that I could of saved someone from drowning, by simply grasping their hand, but I didn't
Instead, I just looked away!

What if you noticed that I am a Christian, but do not witness about what Jesus has done for me...
Instead, I meet the unsaved, and just look away!

It's just as obvious that we must witness, as it is obvious that we could help prevent the bad things listed above, or at least attempted!

When we are saved, we carry the gospel seeds, to disperse; we are to plant them, and try to give others an understanding of what it means to be saved from the most horrible place!

IF

If you are a true believer, then you become a receiver
If you are a receiver, then you are a hearer
If you are a hearer, then you should be a doer
If you are a doer, you should seek to be a reaper
If you are a reaper, then you will be a "praisor"

THE GREATEST CHEERLEADER OF ALL TIME

Lucifer, satan, the devil, cheered as one third of God's angels went with him out of Heaven's splendor

He was glad to have them with him, then and forever

He cheered at the fact that they'll not sing "Worthy is The Lamb", as they admire

Satan cheers at the fact that one day those angels will be thrown in the lake of fire

Lucifer, God's enemy, cheered as Eve and Adam ate of the forbidden fruit in the Garden of Eden

Lucifer cheered and chanted at God that he will always try to get even

Satan cheered as Adam and Eve received punishment and were put out of that beautiful garden

The devil was so happy that they committed sin

Oh, how he cheers all the wicked men of all the ages

Satan cheers at all the wicked and evil things recorded in the Bibles' pages

He cheers from deep within his darkened self

Oh, how he cheers when people choose to ignore God and exalt self

Satan cheered as Judas betrayed Jesus, and how he later hung himself to die, and go to hell

Oh, how he cheered when Judas over-looked The Everlasting Well

Lucifer cheered as Jesus suffered and died on the cross

He cheered at what he wanted: for Jesus' life to be a permanent loss

Lucifer cheers over each hard hearted person

He cheers whenever someone gets deeper in sin

Satan cheers when folks have hatred, anger, bitterness, disunity and pride

He cheers whenever a soul holds on to religion, because they choose to believe a lie

Oh, how he cheers over each backsliding Christian

Satan cheers when good, godly homes and churches are troubled from within

He cheers whenever God's children entertain wicked thoughts and give in to temptations he sends

That devil cheers when our will he bends

Lucifer cheers each day we don't read our Bible and pray

He cheers when we leave God out of just one day

Satan cheers each time we hold on to our anger

He cheers each time we fail to witness to a stranger

Lucifer cheers every time we choose to be in the flesh

He laughs in our face whenever we're in a spiritual mess

Satan cheers each time people don't repent

He cheers each moment hell opens for more souls that are sent

Satan is cheering...do you hear him?

He is cheering with your every sin!

But, as often and loud as he cheers through time...

Within a Christians' heart lives The Greatest Cheerleader of all time!

Who is cheering for you the most?

Is it satan, or is it The Holy Ghost?

WE NEED TO TURN BACK TO GOD

Fellow Christians, gradually something terrible has been happening...

And, when The Lord convicted me, it left me burdened, saddened!

The more I read His precious Word, the more I see that us Christians are not living by and obeying it...

How can Christians read His Word, and not become convicted by The Holy Spirit?

Brethren, we must daily encourage one another...

We must exhort, rebuke and admonish each other!

We need to turn back to God, and His ways...

One by one, we must obey Him, and live for Him, in these last days!

Jesus paid the ultimate price...

So, at the very least, can't we be a "living sacrifice" ?

MY DAYS ARE NUMBERED

My life is but a vapour, the Bible does say

This means that quickly my life is fading away

That is, this life here on earth cannot always last

And, this fact puts my obedience and faith to the test

What test? you may wonder

The same one that's given to all my "sisters" and "brothers"

Since I've been saved, and started growing in The Lord

He has shown me what I'm really on earth for

I must, in His strength, make each day count for His glory

I must give out the gospel, in prayer about hearing another testimony

I haven't a clue, when my life will be over

So, I'll live each day realizing the fact that my days are numbered

I'M NOT WAITING FOR EVERYONE ELSE

Since I've been born again, my life's been rearranged

People look upon me now, as being peculiar and strange

Fellow Christians sometimes persecute my Godly convictions

But, they just don't realize my spiritual condition

I've been commanded by my Master to stand courageously and boldly, in His Name

He has told me to be careful, trying to not bring Him any shame

He has ordered my steps in His Word

And, of what He has said to me, I'm absolutely sure
He has told me to flee from sin, pride and the things that He hates
And flee I do, but only by His grace
As I share with others what He has taught me, I find that many stand still
I cannot understand why they ignore God's Word and will
I cannot put these convictions up on a shelf
I'm not waiting for everyone else!

THIS DAY IS MINE

When I was a newborn Christian, I didn't quite understand some things
I didn't understand that I should seek to be as a "puppet", letting Jesus control the "strings"
I would wake up and think, "this day is mine"
And, I'd do as I pleased, leaving Jesus behind
But, praise God for convicting me that I'm not my own, I am His possession
He showed me that I must live for Him, and to Him draw the attention

As a growing Christian, I try in His strength to live for Him and bring Him pleasure
I must not "float" about in this world as a "feather"
Sometimes in the mornings, on the days things don't seem to go as I'd planned
Satan laughs and says, "this day is mine, even though you're not eternally damned"
But, before I listen to his threats, Jesus tells me with His Still, Small Voice that satan is lying
And Jesus says, "I created this day, it's mine!"

ALL YOURS

Jesus found me and showed me through His Word just how He purchased my salvation
Through the power of The Holy Spirit, I faced interrogation
I saw myself as He saw me, and I knew I needed to trust in Him to save me
He showed me that through His shed blood I could be saved and live in Heaven with Him,
     eternally
He said, "I'm all yours!"
I turned from myself and my sin to bow before Him and be saved
I'll never ever forget that wonderful day!
But, another day, I won't forget, either
It was the day He convicted and challenged me to have "Christian fever"
He said, "I'm all yours, won't you be all Mine?"
I said, "Yes, Lord!", and since then, He convicts me to follow Him, leaving my own desires behind

DROP THE NETS AND GO

MARK 1:15-38

Reflecting upon The Word of God, I think about Simon, Andrew, James and John

They were toiling, fishing with nets, when Jesus invited them to be soul winners; at His invitation, their fellow fishermen thought, "how quickly they're gone"

There was no hesitation

They moved immediately following the invitation

They didn't suggest that they should pray about it

They heard the voice of Jesus and were obedient

When conviction fell upon each one's heart

He was following Jesus, and He didn't have to tell them, "let's start"

My fellow Christians, we are told to walk in The Spirit

Why do many of us continue being disobedient?

When we are toiling, and Jesus speaks in that Still, Small Voice

My friend, there is no need to pray about making a choice

God's will is that we follow and obey Him

Why, after He calls us away from fishing, do we throw the nets out again?

When Jesus gives the word to follow

We should drop the nets and go!

Amen, Hallelujah, this includes me!!

Praise God, with His help, I'll drop my net, and turn away from the sea!

WHEN YOU KNOW JESUS

Since I first met Jesus, He has been gradually affecting my thoughts, actions and feelings; continually molding me into the best I can be, for Him...

I am aware that this is going to be a work-in-progress 'til my time has come

I have met many people who say they're Christians

They say that Jesus has touched them, too, and changed them...

It breaks my heart to see them claim Him, and then turn right back to their sin

I pray that when others are around me that they clearly see that I know Jesus, for real

And, if they look strangely at me as I cringe at evil, I hope they see that I'm not interested in things that don't glorify my Lord

People ask, "How do you live this way, how do you do it?"

I reply, "Because I know Jesus, He gives me the strength to do all things!"

FULL TIME WORK

I have a job which has no time clock, because I never punch out

You see, when I asked Christ to live in my heart, He came, without a doubt

And, since He is now part of me

I am an ambassador for Him, automatically

He washed away all of my sins and unrighteousness

And made me worthy of being one of His representatives

I am honored that He put such responsibility on me

All because I saw Him and fell at His feet in faith, surrender and belief!

He saved me from burning eternally

Therefore, I will try, humbly, to follow through with the responsibilities He lays before me

There is a quote in the Bible that rings true: Therefore if any man be in Christ, he is a new
creature: old things are passed away; behold, all things are become new.

You see, I once was working for a different boss, unaware, unknowingly...

But, when I accepted Jesus, I automatically passed His job interview, and He put me to work,
regardless of my past history!

A VOICE WITHIN

PROVERBS 1:23, 3:6 JOHN 14:16-17

You say that you know Jesus; that His Spirit dwells in you

That is wonderful news!

But, be reminded of something

His Holy Spirit dwells within us when we're saved, right?

And His Spirit is a Voice within us, telling us not to choose wrong, but right...right?

Well, shouldn't we stay tuned in? Do we not check our answering machines when they
have a blinking light?

There is always a message in waiting, for us to notice, from The Holy Spirit, within...

And, if we pay attention to it and follow the direction He tells us to go...there...we find a blessing!

MY JESUS

Once upon a time

Before I knew Jesus was all mine

I struggled and toughed life out

Never realizing what it was all about

I was just another stressed face in the crowd

But, now that I live, knowing Jesus, like a sore thumb, I stand out!

I know I am close to my Jesus

If I'm not doing what the crowd is

Just as soon as I start feeling comfortable around this kind

I stop and re-examine myself, and Jesus brings a message of conviction to my mind!

I have no problem living my life for Him, and being called the odd-ball or labeled different

Because Jesus is bringing my odd-ball self along life's journey, and the rewards I'll reap one day
   will be more than worth it!

A SEED OF DESIRE

Dear Lord, I humbly come to Your Throne of Holiness

Just for a moment, I wish to be a requesting guest

My Bible says that I can come to You in Jesus' Name, about anything

So, Lord, each eve, when I lay to sleep

I wish for You to plant a seed of desire to grow deep

And, I wish for it to grow and sprout before each dawn

So that when I awaken I am overcome with a desire to bring glory to Your Name all day long

Oh, God, I love You so...

That I desire to continuously let it show

My flesh is weak, but my faith is strong

So, Lord, I bring my faith before you and seek a nightly seed of desire to flourish in me and
   help me do right and not wrong

Thank You, Lord, for the chance to come before You

And, thank You for Jesus, because without Him, my prayers would never get through!

SENSITIVE TO SIN

JAMES 1:2-5

Oh precious, Holy Lord

I come to Your Throne, once more

What I am seeking to gain seems so simple

Yet, I ask anyway, because I wish to be completely humble

Lord, please cause me to be so sensitive to sin

That I'm filled with Your Spirit so much that I don't give in to the temptation

Lord, I seek to be so sensitive to sin, that I can "smell" temptation from a "mile" away

Precious Lord, I pray for You to freshen this sensitivity every day

Holy Lord, stand guard at the "gate" of my flesh
And keep Your Holy Spirit strong in my mind, heart, and soul; continuously anew and refreshed
Dear Lord, cause me to be so sensitive to sin
That the very word "sin" causes me to shudder, within
In the Name of Jesus I present this request
Because, for You, I wish to be my very best!

HOW TO SERVE YOU

Lord, after all You've done for me
If I don't do something for You, shame on me!
Lord, is there anyone I can visit, on Your behalf?
Is there an encouraging word, from You, that to others I may pass?
Lord, is there a lonely soul You'd have me to befriend?
Is there a comforting word, from You, I can send?
Lord, is there a child who needs to feel loved?
Is there a way I can show them of Your love, above?
Lord, is there a person in a hospital or nursing home who needs to be cheered?
Is there someone who needs help praying through times of doubt or fear?
Lord, who needs to be told of Your mercy and grace?
May I have the pleasure of telling them, face to face?
Lord, is there a saint who could be touched by a word of praise, or a song?
May You help me praise You and invite others to sing along?
Lord, is there one life I can touch, for Your glory?
Help me count the ways that I can serve You, after all You've done for me!

HELP ME NOT NEED, BUT GIVE

Dear Father,

   First, I'd like to thank You that I'm no longer in need of salvation! You provided it for me, and in my heart, I know You abide! Help me to give to others the wonderful news of salvation You offer them, too!

   Thank You, Lord, for the truth I read in Your Word! I'm glad to have Your wisdom only just a reach away, right in the pages of my Bible. Help me to continually feast upon Your Word, that I may share with others what You say.

   Praise be to You, for being such a good Friend to me! By Your grace, draw my heart to always desire to be at Your side, in fellowship, sweet. Help me to not be in need of having to get back to You, but, rather, to stay close and reach out, inviting others to have fellowship, too.

Father, help me when I have a need to quit being grumpy and stagnant! Help me, instead, to be full of Your Spirit and love, to share a smile and uplifting words with others. Help me to lift others up, instead of being the one who needs all the lifts. Help me to share the love and joy with others that You share with me!

God, help me to make any kind of difference, for Your Name's sake, before my life, a vapour, enters eternity!

Love,
Your Child

FOLLOW THAT WHICH IS GOOD

When choices arise, I look up to my Father

He whispers to my heart, "pray before you go any farther"

After petitions I make

He shows me which choices to choose, which paths to take

Jesus says, "Follow that which is good."

He adds, "read and obey My Word, like you know you should"

Jesus says, "It is good to do what I command."

He reminds me, "the whole time, I'll be holding your hand"

Jesus says, "It is good to bear the fruit of My Spirit in My strength."

He adds, "I'll run the race through you, the whole length."

Jesus tells me, "submit your all to Me, for this is good for you to do"

Then I say, "Yes, Master! I love, worship and praise You!!"

THINGS I WONDER ABOUT

The longer I'm saved, the more curious I become

I frequently wonder why God loved us enough to give us His only begotten Son

I wonder why God would love creatures so unlovable and full of pride

Why did Jesus love us enough to agonize and die?

I wonder about God's love, that will remain a mystery...

Until Heaven I reach, and the answers I finally will see!

The longer I read God's Word, the more amazed I am

I wonder why God's thoughts of me are more numerous than the oceans' grains of sand

At times I wonder just what God is thinking about me

Is He thinking of all that He would have me to be?

I wonder about God's numerous thoughts, are they happy or sad?...

I can't wait to find out, when I finally meet my Heavenly "Dad" !

The more I think about Heaven, the more questions fill my head:
I wonder why God bottles our tears? Who will be my neighbor? Why was I down certain
      paths, led?
I wonder what Jesus will look like, how big will the pile of crowns laid at His feet be?
What will be going on at the "crystal" sea?
I wonder how loud Heaven's choir will sing; Which Bible character I'll meet first, after being
      with my sweet Jesus, Heavens' Light...
What will I see, when my faith finally becomes sight?

Oh, just wondering gets me so excited...
I'm so glad for the moment Jesus' Spirit came to me, and to Heaven, I was invited!

SHOWER OF FORGIVENESS

We all get dirty and take a shower to clean ourselves
We do this to feel better, smell better and to get rid of viruses, germs and everything else
We could not get clean, without soap and water
If we have no soap and water, why bother?
If we were to neglect this daily task, our body would smell fowl
Well, just as sure as we get rid of germs and grime on our outside person
We have an inner person that needs to be washed again and again
Sometimes sins collect in even a saved persons' soul
And, if we don't wash up these sins, the germs will grow out of control
We must take a shower and wash with the soap of Jesus' forgiveness
And rinse with the water of His Word, to cleanse the filth in our hearts, in an effort to keep
      them pure

GIVING THE DEVIL PERMISSION

If you do not submit yourself to The Lord
You're giving the devil permission to torture you some more
Every time you go to the Lord, and leave with doubt
You're giving the devil permission to turn your faith about
Every time you stray from the light of the Lord, and sin
You are giving the devil permission to, in your life, move his darkness back in
Every time you dwell on a negative thought or begin complaining

You're giving the devil permission to find the peace the Lord gave you, and begin draining
Every time you refuse to open the door of your will, to let the Lord inside
You're giving the devil permission to slip in the back door, to find your mind and with it confide
Every time you do not speak and act as the Lord wants you to act
You are giving the devil permission to come near you and begin attack
Every moment that you are unaware...
Beware, because the devil is always out there
You could avoid giving the devil so much permission
By surrounding yourself with scripture, songs and shows that promote being a Christian!

MY ABUNDANT GOD

God has an abundance of mercy, for this He showed to me
I was wicked, lost in sin, but because of His abundant mercy, He cleansed me without and within
He could have let me die and go to hell, with no hope of escape
But, He showed me mercy and then abundant grace
His abundant mercy kept back my due punishment
Then, His abundant grace saved my soul, making my due punishment non-existent
Then He filled my soul with an abundance of joy that will remain as the ages roll
The joy brought an abundance of praise that will last 'til my dying day
The praise brought an abundance of thank yous, for my God shows me love and truth
The thanks led to an abundance of worship in my heart to the God that gave me a new start
This worship leads to an abundance of His Spirit within me, that changes me for all to see, so
    that they, too, may be free
Each day that goes by, abundant blessings are sent to me, from my Father, on High
As our Abundant God is blessing, can't we do an abundant amount of witnessing?

Chapter Eight

Pathway for the Family

..but as for me and my house, we will serve the Lord. Joshua 24:15b

A MARRIAGE BETWEEN TWO

A marriage between two, instead of three

Is not complete, but, rather, insufficient and at times, lonely

You see, each husband and wife must be joined by more than just their wedding vows

They need a Third Person, The Lord Jesus' presence, to fill their house!

WE NEED EACH OTHER

Elders, Seniors, we need you to pray, to be examples of strong faith in The Lord, and to pass
down His Word to the next generation!

Mommies, Daddies, Friends of such age, we need you to take responsibility, pass the torch of
The Lord's Word and plant it in the youth, that it may take root in their hearts!

Youth, we need you to pay attention and be obedient to the Words of The Lord, which are
passed on from your elders...and remember that one day YOU will be the elders!

Everyone, take responsibility and try to walk the way The Lord wishes, and be sure to spread
His Word to each generation!

WEDDING VOWS

MATTHEW 19:6 & EPHESIANS 5:31

I ----- take thee, -----, to be my wedded "spouse"

To have and to hold, from this day forward

For better, for worse

For richer, for poorer

In sickness and in health

To love and to cherish, 'til death do us part

According to God's Holy Word

And thereto, I give thee all my worldly goods

You are now husband and wife!
Kiss your bride, and keep doing so through the years!
Reverence your groom, and keep doing so through the years!

BLESSED HANDS

When I was a little child, I remember getting boo-boo's
My parents would reach out to me, saying, "May I help you?"
I showed them the spot, and ointment and a band aid was applied
Their hands lovingly bandaged my wounds, as they eased my cries
Blessed hands were theirs, that took such good care of me
Blessed hands, to me, they will always be

Growing up, I'd see calluses and cuts on my father's hands, so big to me
He worked so hard, so that we'd be fed and clothed, and have a nice place to sleep
I sometimes thought they looked unsightly
But, then I remembered that they were like that because of me
Blessed hands, my father's hands were to me
Blessed hands, to me, they will always be

Many hours I spent with my mother, in the kitchen
Her hands were always working, sewing, doing dishes, and cooking
She didn't have beautiful nails, with soft, supple skin
She had hands that stayed working and serving
Blessed hands, my mother's hands were to me
Blessed hands, to me, they will always be

On my wedding day, his hands embraced mine
Putting a ring on my finger, to last for all time
How tender and sweet his hands looked; how great it was to give him a wedding ring
His hands looked so handsome, holding the microphone, as for me he did sing
Blessed hands, my grooms hands were to me
Blessed hands, to me, they will always be

What a wonderful day, when my babies were born, and we finally got to meet
How precious they were, from head to feet
But, as their tiny hand grasped my finger
My heart melted, this I'll always remember

Blessed hands, my sons hands were to me
Blessed hands, to me, they will always be

My husbands' hands now look like my father's
And mine look like my mother's
And, every now and then, I hear my kids say
Why do your hands look this way?
I hope that one day they'll say, "Blessed hands, yours are to me"
"Blessed hands, to me, they will always be!"

The hands of my pastor stretched out to me as he started to pray
And as he prayed, God comforted me and showed me the way
Many times, his hands hold a black-back Bible, as God's Word he teaches
And God strips me of fear, and convicts me, as with hands stretched out, he preaches
Blessed hands, my pastors have been to me
Blessed hands, to me, they will always be

Best of all, was the day I needed a Saviour
I needed a way to Heavens' shore
Two nail-pierced hands reached down, for mine
I reached out, too, and salvation I did find
Blessed hands, my Saviour's hands were to me
Blessed hands, to me, they will always be!

PLEASE FORGIVE ME

MARK 11:25-26

I'll never act perfect, or have my words just right
Until after I have taken my Heavenly flight!
So, until then, all I can do is try
And, when I do falter, don't be so surprised!
In my moments of error, due to weakness
All I know to do is truly repent and seek forgiveness!

THANKS A BUNCH!

TO THOSE WHO ARE A BLESSING TO ME AND MY FAMILY

The Christian school teachers that invest their heart, time and love in my children are
    appreciated
Thank you for the many hours of lecturing, and grading papers; and for not showing how
    much you really were agitated

Thank you, Sunday school teachers, as you've studied and prayed as you prepared to teach my
    children, husband and me
Thank you for allowing The Lord to use you to speak to our family

To my pastor, who faithfully serves God, prays for and guides us
Thank you for your listening ear, godly advice and for extra prayers for me the times I am in a mess

To the evangelists I've had the privilege to meet and hear
Thank you for filling my heart with God's Word, and for your testimonies I still hold dear

To the missionaries I've met over the years
Thank you for sharing your ministry, for praising God, for your encouragement, your laughter,
    your tears

To my dear brothers and sisters in Christ, thank you for also touching my life in so many ways
Thanks a bunch, for your testimonies, prayers, words fitly spoken, fellowship and songs of praise

KEEP OPEN COMMUNICATIONS

Something that we all stride to do in life is to keep open communications with those we know
We eagerly share our concerns and problems with them, and encourage them to do the same
    when they are feeling low
Any psychologist or counselor would recommend that you communicate with those you love,
    and, even with yourself
I'll assume that we all stride toward communicating with others somewhat, but, sadly, we can leave
    out the most important Person, leaving Him to watch us communicate with everyone else
If' we'd only realize that He Whom we tend to leave out is the waiting to commune with our
    very soul
He is Jesus, and sadly, many of us tune out His convictions within us, spoken by The Holy Ghost
Even the most spiritual people need to have open communications with their Saviour
For, it is when we have open communications with Him Who resides within us
That we are fully prepared to communicate with others, and avoid many a fuss

THINK ON THESE THINGS

PHILIPPIANS 4:8

Lord, help me to look at my spouse with loving eyes, as You do
Help me to repel negative thoughts, and to think on things that are true
Help me to think on things that are honest and just
Thank You for showing me that thinking on these things is a must
Help me to think thoughts that contain virtue and praise
Throughout all of my married days!

BE RESOLVED

1CORINTHIANS 9:27

Resolve to shun evil thoughts about your mate
Resolve to focus on their good points, with each new day
Resolve to not complain to them
Resolve to forgive, when they do sin
Resolve to speak in warm, loving tones
Resolve to keep peace in your home
Resolve to only speak to others about your spouse in positive ways
Resolve to offer them daily compliments and praise
Resolve to show tenderness and kindness
Resolve to give them unconditional love, coupled with friendliness
Resolve to laugh with them each day
Resolve to be a blessing to them, in numerous ways
Resolve to be the best spouse you possibly can
Resolve to do so, until you're in Heaven's fair Land!

WHO CAN YOU CHANGE?

I've been guilty in the past of trying to change my spouse
I thought that my words of harsh rebuke would turn them around
In my mind, I knew I could cause them to do things differently
Until You, Lord, opened my blinded eyes and let me see
All the while, I needed to work on myself, not my mate
Both of us need to be pliable, for You to mold and shape
I realized that I am not responsible to play the part of The Holy Spirit, and nag
For, in doing so, I was causing You to lag

Since I've stayed out of the way, praying, and waiting
I've seen You move with power, a new person You're creating
Not only do I see You changing my spouse
You're changing me, and the spirit in our house!

I've learned that I can change no one other than myself
I've learned that when I notice fault in others, to trust in You, and close my mouth

PRIORITIES

Lord, help me to stay focused on what is important in life
Enable me to do what's right
Let me always remember to put You first in everything I do
Then, my spouse, at a close number two
Enable us to serve You together
Help us stay close to You, in all kinds of weather

I desire to have priorities, to daily fulfill
Like reading my Bible, praying, and seeking The Lord's will
It's a priority to show love to those in my household
It's a priority to be hot for The Lord, not lukewarm or cold
It's a priority to be a blessing to others, in different ways
It's a priority to share the gospel with someone each day

INSTINCTS

Would a parent tell their hurting child to comfort their self?
Would they tell them to deal with things on their own, without anyone else?
Of course not, parents have natural instincts
God gave parents the capabilities to deal with many things

Would a parent tell their hungry or thirsty child to find their own food and drink, without
     offering to help?
Would they tell them to provide it for their self?
Of course not, parents have natural instincts
God gave parents the capabilities to take care of many things

Would God ever turn down His children's needs?

Would He ever leave His children drowning in raging seas?

Of course not, that's why He gave us instincts

To know to choose Jesus, to read His Word and pray, so that we can make it through all things

Whenever you are in a time of need

Use your spiritual instincts and read

And God will comfort you, feed you

And provide a way for you to make it through

God will never leave you by yourself, to cry

Use your spiritual instincts, and go to your Father, on High!

Just as children come to their parents for most things

So should we go to our Parent for everything!

WHEN YOU'RE EXPECTING

JOHN 14:2,3

I'd like to make an interesting comparison

I'll compare the feelings of an expectant mother and father to the time of expectation of meeting our Saviour

First, the parents learn the news that they're to expect an arrival; just as Christians learn about Jesus, how He'll arrive again, one day

Just as parents are given a due date, we have The Word of God to show us the signs; parents are aware that their arrival may come sooner or later than expected, so may our Lord come earlier or later than we expect Him

The parents prepare for the arrival, by making room; we must make room in our hearts, and be prepared to meet our Lord

As the expected arrival arrives, what a happy meeting it is, as the parents bask in joy and excitement; Likewise, will God's children have a happy meeting, a glad reunion with their Parent!

MOMS, MAKE A DIFFERENCE

There is nothing more overwhelming to me than the responsibility of being a mom

My children look up to me for the answers to all of their questions, they ask me to help them when they cannot do something, so, I help by giving them suggestions

I cannot scientifically explain why certain things are the way they are, so, I offer my best thoughts, and with their "new" knowledge they walk away, grinning

It is so important to be a positive, godly influence; the way we act when handling our
   situations is how they're most likely to act when they look for their own solutions
It is as equally important to explore their world and listen to their thoughts, showing them
   respect, too; after all, they are people with feelings, like me and you
We should teach patience, honesty, respect, faithfulness, good manners, humbleness and
   Christianity
It's our job to motivate them and encourage them, and to also correct and discipline them
The test results of how we've done will come in someday, when they're out in the world, on
   their own
Even then, we should be available, for when they have times of confusion, lacking wisdom
However we raise them, we need to know that the seeds we sew will grow, the bad as well as
   the good
Mommies, beware, and take care of the ones God has entrusted in your care!

DRESS YOUR BEST
GALATIANS 6:3

Each morning, we skim over our wardrobe and pull out the most appealing pieces to put on
We iron them to perfect them, and step in front on a mirror to tidy up some more, but never
   realize what we've forgotten!

Everything looks pleasing to us, in that mirror, even the expression cast upon our face
But, how can we be dressed our best, if we haven't yet reflected on God's grace?

It does not matter the most whether we have our shirt ironed or tucked in
What others notice the most, including our Lord, is what we expose from within!

If we would only stride to live as our Lord wished, looking into the mirror of His Word,
   seeking Christian behavior
We could be dressed our best in even second-hand attire!

THE TONGUE
JAMES CHAPTER 3

The tongue can no man tame
It can offer love, praise, hatred and shame
We are each accountable for what ours says, we bear the blame!

HELP ME TO BE THE SAME
JAMES 1:8

Thank You Lord, for refreshing my soul each time I go to a church service

I appreciate the good singing, the testimonies, the preaching and sharing my prayer requests

How great it is to get along so good with my sisters and brothers

I enjoy the fellowship we have with one another

The hugs from the little ones are priceless

My heart breaks as the pastor preaches, and my sins I confess

There's no other place on earth I'd rather be than in church service, worshipping You

Every time I go, You show me something new

But, Lord, when Monday comes, there's no service to attend

Help me to stay focused on You, and time with You spend

Help me to enjoy good singing, testimonies and time in prayer at home

Whether I do so with others, or all alone

Help me to get along with my family, just as I do with my brethren, on Sundays

Help me to create times of fellowship with them on non-church days

Help me to get plenty of priceless hugs from my own little ones

Help me to apply what my pastor preached about, and still confess my sin

Help me to daily ask You for forgiveness, and not wait until Sunday to look within

Help me to make my home the happiest place on earth, where we worship You

Help me to be the same as I am on Sunday when Monday comes, and the whole week through!

JUST BE CONTENT
HEBREWS 13:5 & PROVERBS 15:27

Lord, as I look to my neighbor at my left and to my right

I see that they have things that are nice

I look across the street, and around the block

And, I notice the great things they've got

Then, as I gaze upon what I have, you say, "Just be content!"

Help me, Lord, to always be thankful to You

Help Thou me to be grateful for salvation and Your truth

Help me show that I appreciate the family I have

I need Your help, Dear Lord, to be pleased with today's blessings, never looking back

Help me, Lord, to look up, within, and around, and meditate on the truth in Your Word, and
just be content!

HELP ME BE HUMBLE
2CHRONICLES 7:14

Lord, when I think things are tough, and begin to grumble

Help me to keep my mind stayed on Thee, and be humble

Lord, when I begin to think that I'm above a certain task at hand

Help me remember what You did for me, and humbly obey Your command

Lord, when I feel as though I have no more to give

Help me to reach out to others, and try to be a blessing each day I live

Lord, help me to not look down on anyone

Help me to be humble, always aware that I'm better than no one

GRANDPARENTS ARE SPECIAL PEOPLE

Grandparents are special people, you see

They have knowledge and wisdom that they happily share with me!

They are always busy giving their love

As well as passing down lessons learned throughout their life about how to be closer to The
    Lord, above!

They always have a cookie jar for me to snitch from

And a shoulder for me to cry on!

They encourage me to do good things

No matter how near or far they are, they're always tied to my heart-strings!

They share their pride with me when I do right, and celebrate with me all of the happy
    occasions of my life

They have a way of showing unconditional love; I know if I mess up in life that they'll still
    keep their love and support by my side!

They have shown so many things to me

But, most importantly, how to spread love evenly over an entire down line of family!

HUSBANDS AND WIVES

So many husbands stride to have a perfect lawn

But, do they stride to have a perfect marriage?

So many husbands seek to know all they can about sports stats

How many of them know about their wife's likes, dislikes, favorite color, flower, etc.?

So many husbands give all they've got to their golf swing

But, do they give all they've got to their wife and children?

So many husbands sit, patiently waiting all day for a few nibbles at the hook of their fishing rod
But, how many of them take that patience home?

So many wives are busy grumbling or complaining
If they'd only speak of good things, they wouldn't be so offending
So many wives are too busy cooking, cleaning and sweeping the floor
That they ignore those whom they're doing it for
So many wives disrespect their man
And then they don't understand why they later have to chase him down, and beg, just to hold
    hands
So many wives bring a negative spirit into their home
And then don't realize that they started the problem on their own!

SIDETRACKED

Satan has so many ways to distract Christians
He has so many different ways to keep Christians from "Christian" living
He knows what to tempt us with, what pleases us, that is, our flesh
Then, God allows him to persecute, as in the days of Job, but, sadly, many of us fail the test
Christians who could make a world of difference
Are spending most of their time with televisions, sports, selfish activities, and, to God, being
    indifferent
How many Christians are forfeiting family altar
To cheer at a ball game, or sit in front of Hollywood's screen, eating popcorn?
What a shame, how Christians are so easily sidetracked!
What a shame, that when standing before Lord Jesus Christ one day, the hands of time cannot
    be turned back!
What are our children to become?
Spiritual, Godly...unlikely, if they're taught, "I scored the most, I'm number one!"
This grieves The Holy Spirit, touches my heart, and I feel that there is not much I can do
Other than encourage others, fervently pray, and to my God try to be true!

FOR ALL ETERNITY

It's wonderful to be assured by God Himself
That I belong to Him, and no one else
My soul is thrilled at the thought of finally meeting my Saviour
After all, He is Lord of all, Owner of this universe, it's Creator

Oh, how glad I am that my name is in His book of life

But, my joy is turned to sorrow, if I think twice

You see, I'm safe and secure

But there's a burden in the depths of my soul for the "lost" out there

For all eternity, I will be with Lord Jesus

But, for all eternity, they're doomed to hell's flames, and to weep, wail and gnash their teeth as they're tormented in hell's darkness

Oh that Jesus would help me win to the truth my Mom and Dad

Oh, that He would help me win to the truth my grandparents and the siblings I have

The thought of my eternity makes me very happy

Yet, on the other hand, it makes me feel the urgency

It is appointed unto men, to once die

Lord, won't You help me to reach them before it's too late; if not, why?

Lord, search me and know me and see if there be any wicked way in me

Help me to repent and be used for Your own glory

Father, please don't let them perish without an urgent call by The Holy Spirit

Lord, enable me to share, again, the Gospel, and, I beg of You to convict them to believe and receive it

For all eternity, I shall be happy

But, Heaven would be sweeter if the ones I witnessed to were with me!

TOP TEN LIST OF CHRISTIANS EXCUSES

10. I am too angry to stop and pray, I must vent instead

9. God didn't answer my last prayer, so, He must not care

8. It's too early in the day to pray

7. The children aren't interested in learning The Bible

6. How can I lead family altar after working all day?

5. I can't come to church, someone hurt my feelings

4. I can't sing out for Jesus, I'm off key

3. Praying takes too long after a hard days' work

2. It's not quiet enough at my house to read my Bible

1. I have no time to read my Bible, and all that I do is important, and must get done

The author of these, and many more excuses, for you to borrow any time is:

Lucifer, the devil, the anti-Christ, the rebellious, fallen angel, the enemy of Jesus and EVERY Christian!!

Read and pray about 1PETER 5:8

CHRISTIANS OF OLD

The more I study about the Christians of old, the more I grieve

Because most Christians of this day have turned to the world, and no longer clearly see!

Many Christians of old burned at the stake for trying to win souls

While many today are popular for scoring so many sports-related goals!

What stench in the nostrils of God!

That "modern" Christians no longer are consecrated to their first Love!

The Christians of old were convicted, diligent, and stood up for, lived by and died for The
     Holy Bible

But, today, is there only a handful of Christian homes with consistency, love for righteousness
     and a deep desire for genuine revival?

NO MORE THINKING TWICE

PSALMS 32:8

So many times in our lives, we come to decisions, and find ourselves second guessing

We go through a phase of questioning ourselves and reasoning

We weigh out the pro's and con's, and each possible choice, and choose the one with the
     strongest "voice"

If we only knew that there is a way to make decisions, without all these frustrations

It is a fact that if we know Jesus , then all we need to do is listen for His Still, Small Voice, and
     follow, with our behavior

For, it is only when we know Jesus, and listen to His Voice that we won't have to think twice

CHOOSE YOUR FRIENDS WISELY

If you're a Christian, choose Christian friends to spend time with

Choose those who are godly, good-spirited and quick to forgive

Choose friends who are seeking God's face

Choose friends who will encourage you to keep running your race

Choose friends who are honest, honorable and humble

Choose friends who will help you up when you stumble

GOOD CALL, REF'

I like to think of Jesus as the "Referee" of my life

When this world scores against me, causing me sorrow or strife

I wait patiently for the "Referee" to sound His whistle

And tell me that I have a few shots to be forgiving and peaceful

So, having been told, I follow, and soon find myself calm, as I catch my breath

And, I realize that He was right, and give praise by saying, "Good call, Ref' "

Sometimes when this world scores against me, by trying to sweep my children away

The "Referee" blows His whistle, for me to have a time out, to kneel and pray

So, I find myself kneeling and praying for them not to be swayed by the ways of this world

And, as I finish praying, here is my child knocking upon my door

I realize that this is a moment I must seize

To tell my child, again, about the goodness of Jesus

And, I see that my child is under conviction, and curiously asking questions, not even taking time for a breath

So, I stop and tell The Lord thanks, for hearing my prayer, then I give thanks for the time out I had to pray, and offer praise by saying, "Good call, Ref' "

A CHRISTIAN HOME

ROMANS 12:1; EPHESIANS 6:13; COLOSSIANS 3:1-2,17; 1TIMOTHY 4:12

Many claim to run a Christian home

And, without realizing it, may be allowing room in it for the devil to roam

The word "Christian" can be broken into two parts

The first is "Christ", we know Him, if He lives in our hearts

The second, "-ian" means of, relating to or resembling

When we put them together, it's interesting

When someone's born again

They're of Christ, related now to God, by adoption, and the resemblance soon begins

If we run a Christian home

The Spirit of Christ should be welcome, and He should freely roam

We have radios, televisions and other things to entertain us

But, remember, this is the same entertainment we're offering Jesus

Many programs have violence, anger, pride, and sexual, suggestive scenes here or there

If we spend time with them, we absorb it, perhaps even unaware

Even songs send suggestive, ungodly messages that pierce our minds and hearts

Jesus pleads with us to not give it a chance to start

We must be extremely cautious about what we allow in our homes

If Jesus doesn't approve of something, why give the devil a little room in which to roam?

Everything is not pleasing to The Lord

We must keep Jesus in mind when using computers, radios or televisions- ask Him to inspect everything before carrying it through our door

We are called to be holy, to be ambassadors, representatives for Christ

Our home ought to give this indication, by those living inside

Be challenged to give up what's not right, and to set the tone for Jesus to happily live with you

And others will notice that God gets the glory in how you live and in what you say and do

Play programs and background music that glorifies Christ, for one whole day...

And you will sense the presence and joy of The Lord, and you'll want to keep it that way!

If you're afraid to make even a small sacrifice

Realize that you're taking satan's advice

Some things in your home, The Lord wouldn't hold on to for a minute

Be challenged to toss them aside; you'll not regret it!

Since you're a Christian, choose to run your home as Christ would have you to

Stand at every outlet and entrance, to keep the devil from getting through

Can you imagine Jesus asking satan to entertain Him, and visit for a while?

Try the spirits, be cautious of satan's many profiles!

Remember what we're looking at and listening to

We're causing Jesus to, too!

And, if He doesn't find it entertaining, interesting or funny, as we may...

Perhaps we should acknowledge that satan's in the process of leading us away!

Get ready, if you kick the devil and his forms of entertainment out of your domain...

Because he will work overtime, through others, and mock, in hopes that you'll abandon your decision and let him in again!

WHAT'S WRONG WITH OUR YOUTH?
PROVERBS 29:15,17

Us, the parents, see how our children and teens are behaving, and wonder, "what's wrong?"

We notice their bad attitudes, negative comments, and their faces look so long

They seem to live for self, seeking the treasures this world has to offer

We wonder if guiding them will be worth the "bother"

Parents, we must recognize that part of the problem rests on us

Training, advising and guiding them is a must

If we neglect the rod of discipline, and the duty of reproof, they will lack wisdom

Perhaps we are partly to blame for their being spiritually ho-hum

Are we spending time in The Bible with them? Praying with them?

Are we reprimanding, strongly warning and restraining them? Are we showing a balance of
discipline and love to them?

God says that if we leave them to themselves, they will bring us shame, especially the mother

Especially she must nurse, nurture and teach them, with fervor

Without shouting and condemning them, we ought to correct them and teach God's ways

A lot of times, they mimic the way we behave

If we walk close with The Lord, and close to our youth

Perhaps so many of them would not go aloof

Parents: love, nurture, discipline and train

Youth: learn, obey, respect; and, wisdom you'll gain

WHAT I'M THANKFUL FOR

I'm thankful for being born in a free country

For having parents who lovingly raised me

For a mother who fed me, washed me, inspired me

For a father who provided for my needs, who laughed with and guided me

For siblings that shared hours of play

For the memories we shared each day

For the loving words of wisdom I heard my grandparents say

For loved ones and strangers, friends and teachers who encouraged me along life's way

I'm thankful for being married to a Christian man

For living in a Christian home, where God's Word stands

For precious children; even for their kool-aid stained lips and dirty little hands

For the good times, the bad times, the times I felt, "I can't" and the times I felt, "I can"

I'm thankful for a good church to go to

For having God's Word, Spirit, and a good Pastor to help me through

For brethren, friends and neighbors, too

But, most of all, for Jesus, salvation, the way and the truth!

LEMONS OF LIFE

PROVERBS 17:22, PHILIPPIANS 4:8

When you're in the heat of the day, and you long to satisfy your thirst

Refreshing, sweet lemonade, you desire first

It's great with a few ice cubes dancing within

Top it off with sugar or honey, and then let the tasting begin

Sit down, relax, and enjoy what you created from mostly lemons

You may want to offer some to your friends

When you're in the heat of a problem, you've been handed a lemon, and for a solution, you thirst

Refreshing, sweet lemonade, you should desire first

It's great to cool down your frustration within

Top that off with kindness and sweetness, and then let your positive outlook begin

Be still, and encouraged, be creative and enjoy what you can create from lemons

You may want to offer this advice to your friends

Life's hard! Lemons are bitter!

Add some sugar and things will get better!

When dealing with the lemons of life

Don't act bitter, inviting more strife!

TIME OUT FOR MOM AND DAD

PROVERBS 29:15

Children have had enough time out!

It's time for parents to know what time out is about!

Mom, take time out from your chores and daily cleaning

Spend time with your children; for time with you, their hearts are grieving!

Dad, take time out from work, hobbies and the honey do list

Spend time with your children- it's you that they miss!

TOGETHER

ECCLESIASTES 4:9-10

Take time, together, to laugh out loud

Be silly, be goofy, don't be too proud

Go, together, into the beautiful outdoors

Sit, together, reminiscing at a campfire, eating "s'mores"

Together, smell the flowers, look at the stars, feel the rain

Be together in health, wealth, sorrow and pain

Peek in, together, upon the sleeping children

Together, share your hopes and dreams with them

Go, together, to church; be of one accord

Serve, together, do all you can for The Lord

FRIENDS FOR LIFE

I'M THANKFUL FOR MY PARENTS, MY FRIENDS FOR LIFE!

Parents have a special job to do

They must care for their little ones, and lead them in truth

Parents help their children before they can even help themselves

They put what they would rather do on a shelf

Parents are doctors, nurses, teachers, chefs, counselors

Lawyers, personal trainers, encouragers, taxi drivers, correctors for wrong behaviors

Parents are janitors, decorators, bakers

Builders, lecturers

They are painters for bedrooms, landscapers for the lawn

They are shoulders to cry on, help to rely on

Parents lead the way through grief and strife

They share in the good times; they're friends for life!

THROUGH EVERYTHING

Be there for one another each day

Show that you care in different ways

Laugh when they're laughing

Pray when they're crying

Cheer when they're winning

Comfort when they're hurting

Listen when they're speaking
Speak words they're needing
Leave notes of love for them to find
Offer gestures that are tender and kind
Lift them up when they're down
Turn their frowns upside-down
Be there, by their side, in good and bad times
Be faithful to them, when they need you, stop on a dime
Rejoice with them, praise God with them
Study God's Word with them, kneel and pray with them
Be with them through everything!

I NEED HELP

Help me, Lord:
To lose my extra weight
To eat healthy and stay in shape
To spiritually and physically look great

To please You and my mate

IS THERE NOT A CAUSE?
1SAMUEL 17:29, PROVERBS 22:6

Each child has a soul
The battle rages between good and evil, to win control
Parents, teach them as they grow
God's salvation and the High Road, daily show
Is there not a cause?
They're still learning and growing when your guidance is on pause!

BUT AS FOR ME

If you're the only adult serving God in your home
Don't be discouraged, you can serve Him alone
Make up your mind a Christian to be
Stand up and declare, "But as for me!"

Tell satan, "As for me and my corner of the house, I will serve The Lord!"

Daily walk closer with God than the day before

Let your service be on open display

After taking time to secretly pray

Lift up Jesus

And He will draw others!

WHAT GOD SAYS ABOUT TRUE LOVE
1CORINTHIANS CHAPTER 13

God's Word says that if I speak all languages, or like an angel, I sound like an annoying tune
without harmony, if I have not love

If I understand prophecies, have great knowledge and faith, but love isn't deep in my heart,
God doesn't need me to do any special service for Him, above

If I give all I have to the poor or die a martyr's death without the true love of God in my heart,
God will not reward me

God says that His love in our heart will cause us to forgive, be patient and loving to others,
even to those who've treated us unjustly

His love in our heart causes us to be kind, not jealous of what others do or have

It causes us to shun pride, to not argue on anyone's behalf

God's love in our heart causes good character, causes us to openly and secretly be a blessing to
others, not expecting recognition or reward

The love of God in our heart causes us to not be angered easily and declare war

It causes us to think good of others, not bad

It causes us to realize when we've done wrong and forsake the bad habits we have

His love in our heart causes us to rejoice in truth

It causes us to keep on keeping on when we're mocked and tempted to be blue

It causes us to believe all of The Word of God whether we understand or not

This love causes us to have the hope that God will hear and answer our prayers, according to
the will of God

The love of God in our heart causes us to not be discouraged, for His love never runs out

It causes us to hear God's Word and not doubt

This love will let us know that we don't know much

Just as there is a difference between us as a child, and now, a grown up

It reassures us that one day we'll see that we aren't all that we think we are

When we meet God, He'll show us how "off the mark" we really are

God's Word declares that it's good to have faith and hope in Him

But, if we lack love, charity, we haven't the greatest trait; faith and hope without love is sin

HINDERED PRAYERS

1PETER 3:1-7

God commands wives to trust in Him, and each one to respect her husband

This calls for a walk with God and daily prayer, without end

He wants wives to be more concerned about personal holiness than appearance or fashion

He wants wives to have a meek and quiet spirit, not to complain to or boss their husbands

He wants maturity and respect to show from the depths of her heart

And, if she's not hearkening, He bids her to start

Then, God says likewise to the man

He says for husbands to offer a loving hand

God commands the husband to show honour to his wife

And not to be a tyrant, but a joint heir together with her, of the grace of life

He calls each husband to be loving, gentle, thoughtful, realizing that when compared to
 himself, his wife is weaker

God says for wives and husbands to obey these words, that their prayers be not hindered

CHILDREN, JUST OBEY

PROVERBS 20:11 AND EPHESIANS 6:1-3

Though you are but a child, God has a call for you

He gives you a job of honoring your parents, and doing what they say to do

God promises to know your heart, and the motive behind your deeds

Please give respect to Mom and Dad, doing so can bring much ease!

Dear children, obey God by respecting and obeying your parents

God says that in doing so, a long life you may inherit!

EXERCISE THYSELF

Running and playing exercises my muscles, and makes me strong, and tough

Playing games and writing exercises my brain, but that isn't enough

Gods' Word says that the most important of all

Is exercise for my spirit and soul!

Reading my Bible every day

And spending time with God, taking time to pray

Exercise my spirit and soul, and teach me how to be godly

And, I do this work-out gladly!

The part of us that needs exercise the most is the part of us that is indwelt by The Holy Ghost!

LITTLE ONES

Children are sent from above
For us to guide, nourish and love
We must shower them with information
About God and His creation
We must enlighten them on what's right and wrong
And encourage them to not just read others' poems and songs, but to also create their own
We need to encourage and motivate them to pray to The Lord about reaching their dreams
We must teach them by our words and actions to do what's right no matter how tempting
    things may seem
To them, we must display unconditional love
So they will know how to one day show it to their little ones sent from above
And, before we know it, they'll be big enough to fill our shoes
And, with their little ones, lead down the path of life as we did and will always offer to do

AN INVISIBLE FATHER

(MY PRAYER, WHEN I WAS A SINGLE MOM FOR A SEASON)

Lord, after so much heartache, stress and pain
I find myself calm, more optimistic than I was just yesterday
But, Lord, I come to You with one great wish
My platter of life seems full, but one thing's missing from my dish
As You know, Lord, the path of my life has taken me to a place I never dreamed I'd be
On my own, to raise three
As You see, Lord, I do all that I can
And, You know, Lord, this was not Your plan
I need a real Father for my children, Lord
One they can always count on, to never walk out the door
I want a Father for them, who's excitedly by my side
Admiring with me, the precious, happy and sad moments, even the moments of peeking in on
    them when they've settled their heavy little eyes
I wish to have a Father lead the way in times I need to show discipline
Lord, when I correct them, they need a Father to lay on them conviction
Lord, I place my faith in You
To make this wish come true
Something's missing, Lord, I feel such a void

I pray that You, Lord, will fill it with Your Fatherly presence, bringing us Your guidance,
    protection and joy
I will faithfully continue being their mother
But, Lord, I need a partner, and my boys need at the very least, an Invisible Father
So, please, Lord, come into my little family and act as the Head
And, I'll follow Your lead with no regret
Thank You, Lord, for understanding the words of this desperate mother
And granting my wish; that my boys and I can always count on their Invisible Father!

A QUICK TESTIMONY

Having grown up in a religious home, attended Catholic School through eighth grade, being confirmed as a teen, I married my boyfriend of four years, gave birth to three sons, in five years of marriage, I found myself grieving, as he had an affair, never coming back home. I was twenty-three years old, without The Lord in my life. Someone persistently invited me to church, and encouraged me to invite God into my life. I refused for months. I even told that person, "I don't need God, I can take care of things on my own!" BUT GOD wouldn't give up on me. I finally gave in and went to church to get this person to leave me alone about coming. I intended to go one time, to hush them up, and then continue doing things my own way, without God! I thought I didn't need God, that somehow I'd manage my problems and heartaches on my own. At the church, I heard things I'd never heard, my heart flipped and flopped within me. At the close of service, the invitation, I went to the altar, crying, my heart about to burst, not exactly knowing why I went forward. Others were there, crying and praying. They shared with me the ONE WAY to Heaven, God's plan of salvation. Until this point, I had only had religion. I never realized what I'd always believed was wrong, until this night. I struggled with this new truth, not knowing exactly what to do with it. The Christians there tried to help me, I'll never forget it! They gave me a Bible and a Christian workbook. I took them home and read and read for months on end, while faithfully attending church. After struggling for eight months, one night while reading God's Word, God opened my heart and my eyes! I trusted Him alone for salvation, with my life, doing a one hundred and eighty degree turn. The sky was prettier, the birds sang sweeter, the grass even seemed greener! I never knew how much God cared for me, how much Jesus cared for me, enough to die in my place, arise and pay my pardon with His blood, to cover MY sins! He took my guilt and shame, replacing it with peace and joy, a brand new start! And, over time, He mended my broken heart. It's been almost eight years since I've been born again, and I am finding that He really is sweeter as the days go by! I've been remarried for seven years; a whole new life I've found!

I'm part of a wonderful, soul-winning, revival-seeking, truth-preaching, bus-reaching, Jesus-worshipping, old-fashion church! The Lord works in my family's life daily! God is Good!!

GARY'S TESTIMONY (MY HUSBAND)

After being married, playing church for a few years, one morning while singing in church, the words of the song I was singing convicted me that I needed to once and for all trust in The Lord for salvation. For some time before this, my wife and three stepchildren were concerned, praying over this very thing. They weren't surprised to see me hit the altar after singing, but many others were. Church members knew me as Brother Gary at church, not knowing the real me, when out of church. They didn't know my areas of struggle, as did my family, in my home life. So, at the altar, they encouraged me that I was already saved, that this day I was just re-dedicating my life to God. In my heart, I knew they were wrong, but I struggled over assurance of true salvation, over knowing for sure if I had called on God in the right way. Months later, when struggling again, my wife called a godly man from our church to come to our home. He encouraged me to kneel and call on The Name of The Lord, specifically asking Him to save me. So, I did. Yet, within time, I struggled again, doubting that God saved me. Within a couple of years, God led us to the church we're currently members of. After hearing solid preaching continuously, and a message on assurance, I started struggling again, worse than before. My wife was very concerned and asked our Pastor to pray for me. After several months, when all answers seemed to fail me, she called him and encouraged me to meet with him. At 9 pm we headed to the church to see if he could help me. He opened the Word of God and showed me what God says about salvation, and assurance thereof. God dealt with my heart, through the preacher's words, and God's Word. On May 30, 2008, I accepted assurance of salvation at 10:30 pm. To sum it up: God said it, I believed it, and that settled it, AMEN!

BRENDAN'S TESTIMONY (OLDEST SON)

I got saved at age 11, on January 29, 2008. I live in a Christian home where we have family devotions regularly. I go to a Christian School, where the Pastor of our church is my teacher. We go to church and hear the Word of God preached every time the doors are open. One night, during devotion, my Mom was talking about how people go to hell if they aren't saved. The Lord grabbed hold of my heart and my Mom called the Preacher, and over the phone, I knelt, as he led me to The Lord. I have been growing in The Lord from different things. Part of the reason, I am in a Godly environment.

PHILIPP'S TESTIMONY (MIDDLE SON)

When I was five years old, one night, I was playing preacher. I was preaching to my Mom, and two brothers. I was preaching on hell, and I got convicted by my own preaching! That is when I realized that I needed to be saved. I talked with God about it, and He took the bad feeling from my heart and tummy. I was very happy and full of joy. The date was April 11, 2003. I live in a Christian home and am trying to live my life for The Lord.

THOMAS' TESTIMONY (YOUNGEST SON)

I got saved when I was seven. It was April 16, 2007. After we prayed in family altar, I found out I wasn't saved, so I wanted to be saved. When I was going to bed after praying, The Lord started dealing with my heart. I knelt beside my bed and asked God to save me. The next morning, I asked Philipp (we share a room) to forgive me for fussing and fighting with him. Then I told my family I got saved. And now, I'm glad to be living in a Godly and Christianly family.

IDEAS FOR FAMILIES

1. Start a family prayer box, removing requests when answered, and thanking God together.
2. Design a peg board or dry erase board, including everyone's favorite scriptures.
3. Let children make pictures for Jesus and God, and hang them.
4. Let children write letters to The Lord, and save them in a special scrap book.
5. Let children design their own Christian tee shirt with paint, etc.
6. Tape record made up songs for The Lord. Listen often.
7. Have children write down their bad behaviors, ask God for help, then throw them in the trash.
8. Make up skits and spend family time acting them out. Teach how to handle tough situations, too.
9. Make construction paper hands, feet, etc. and discuss service for The Lord, being surrendered.
10. You and children write thank yous to church folks, Sunday School Teachers, etc.
11. Make drawings of your Pastor, tell your favorite sermon, silliest memory, etc. and deliver them in person.
12. Make up your own stories; spiritual, silly, and be creative, to teach values and build character.
13. Sing favorite church songs together.
14. Leave "mail" on each other's pillows regularly.
15. Have ice cream with breakfast once in a while, and pancakes for supper. Let the kids serve.
16. Create a missionary poster, board, etc. and look on a map to where they are and pray for them.
17. Pray daily for your pastor and his family.
18. Pray the church's prayer list at home, as a family.
19. Speak positively about church members, rebuking complaints.
20. Write letters and send them to missionaries. Try to get your whole church involved.
21. Make fun schedules for days off, or during summer, and stick to them. Make them as kid-friendly as possible. Include ways to serve The Lord.
22. Play games together, indoors and outdoors as much as possible.
23. Visit nursing homes as a family, letting children distribute pictures they've colored.
24. Buy crazy colored light bulbs and put them in the children's rooms on Friday nights.
25. Make up jokes and fill-in-the-blank stories.

Chapter Nine

Pathway to Eternity

For what shall it profit a man, if he shall gain the whole world, and lose his own soul?   Mark 8:36

LIFE AND DEATH

Life's about laughing, and about crying
Life's about hurting, and about healing
Life's about growing, and about changing
Life's about gaining, and about losing
Life's about mountains, and about valleys
Life's about clear skies, and about cloudy ones
Life's about needing, and about giving
Life's about listening, and about speaking
Life's about seeing, and about believing
Life's about flowers, and about winter
Life's about sunshine, and about rain
Life's about living, and about dying

Death's about eternity, and about souls
Death's about Heaven, or about Hell
Death's about gladness, or about regret
Death's about peace, or about fright
Death's about darkness, or about light
Death's about meeting your Saviour, or about your rejecting behavior
Death's about faith becoming sight, or about unbelief that wishes it were right
Death's about no more chances, or about having no regret
Death's always comes sooner than we are willing to "bet"

WHO

Who loves you, when no one else does?
Who can comfort you, when nothing else does?
Who loves you so much, that He died in YOUR place, so that you may live in Heaven forever?
Who makes it possible for us to see the Face of God?

The One and Only Lord and Saviour, Jesus Christ!

THE GREATEST LOVE, EVER

I thought I had found a love that's true

But, one unexpected day, it was through

I felt so lonely, hurt and blue

I cried from day to day, not knowing what to do

All the while, God was saying, "I love you"

But I didn't listen, I was busy trying to find life anew

I thought if I changed my appearance that someone would love me, but that fell through

My heart ached with loneliness, to find love that really was true

When I was in the depths of despair, God still said, "I love you"

Jesus reached down His hand and asked, "What are you going to do?"

I grabbed His hand, and He pulled me out, to life anew

Since that moment, His love has proved true

He's always with me, and when problems come, He doesn't leave me, but pulls me through

My only regret is not choosing Him the first time He asked me to

My Friend, Jesus, is reaching His hand to you, asking, "What are YOU going to do?"

WHAT ARE YOU DOING?

On Sunday, what are you seeing? Where are you going?

On Monday, what will you do? What will you say?

On Tuesday, where will you eat? When will you sleep?

On Wednesday, what has to be done? What's for fun?

On Thursday, what will you buy? Who will you call?

On Friday, how much will you spend? With whom will you share your time?

On Saturday, how late will you sleep in? What will you do for leisure?

On SOMEDAY, when your life rushes to an end, where will your soul be going? What will your soul be doing?

For help, please read:
Hebrews 9:27
2Corinthians 6:2
Isaiah 1:18
Luke 12:20
John 14:6

JUST THAT QUICK

I was a sinner, on my way to hell

But, now I have a story to tell!

The Spirit of The Lord worked on my heart for some time

But now I am His, and He is mine!

At the final moment, before I was saved, God showed me myself through His eyes

I could no longer hide behind a religious disguise!

One moment I was going to hell, and unknowingly, satan was my friend

But, just that quick, I became a new creation; Jesus became my Friend as soon as I was born again!

Wow! I turned from the path of destruction and eternal damnation

How quickly I was saved, Heaven bound, looking forward to my eternal home...what a celebration!

Dear friend, if you don't have a story like this to tell to others

Then your soul ought to be bothered!

If The Lord pleads with you, it could be your last chance to be set free

Because just that quick, you could enter into your eternity!

AM I GOOD ENOUGH

EPHESIANS 2:8-9

You can be a well behaved person, since the time you were a child

You can be a teen who has never done anything too bad or wild

You can be an adult who always tries to be truthful and good

You can be a good citizen who obeys the laws, as we should

You can devote your life to nursing the sick and feeding the poor

You can do more good things with your life than anyone's ever done before

You can be a devoted parent and faithful to your mate

You can tell others that it's wrong to cheat, steal, lie and hate

You can be the best employee where you're employed

You can give love and kindness to those by whom you could be annoyed

You can be a loving grandparent to your little clan

You can meet a stranger with a need and lend a helping hand

You can be the best friend anyone's ever had

You can honor and respect those who try to make you mad

You can give your money to every charity you hear of

You can adopt orphaned children and give them lots of love

You can run a homeless shelter, providing folks with clothes and food

You can make excuses for people who are mean and crude

You can be a shoulder for people who are hurting and crying

You can defend innocent people from those who are lying

You can be the most loving, forgiving, kind and giving person this world has ever known

You can be a church member who pays tithes and obeys all the rules you're shown

You can be full of hope that some day when you die, you'll surely get into Heaven for being so good

You can say that you always lived as you thought you should

Standing before God one day, when you expect to spend eternity with Him, in Heaven above

When He doesn't let you in, you'll plead, "Am I good enough?"

    Then He will show you that no one ever entered Heaven by simply trying to do their best

God will tell you that only those saved, coming through Jesus' shed blood may enter in, and that He refuses the rest

You will cry that He's not fair, and that you thought He was a loving God

But He will stand firm in the fact that only those may enter in who turned to Jesus, when their soul He sought

God will let you remember that He gave you His Word, The Holy Bible

He will let you think about the Christians He sent your way to explain to you the one way to Heaven, and that you graciously rejected the truth, though

You will admit that your Bible just collected dust

And that you ignored the truth and just lived how you thought you must

You'll remember throwing away the gospel tracts that were put in your hand from time to time

You will remember telling Christians, "I'm not going to visit your church, I only like going to mine!"

You'll see that to Jesus' perfection you never can compare

It'll be too late, but you'll want to accept the truth and be saved and enter, but God will cast you in hell and let you know that your eternal home is there

You'll regret forever and forever that you held on to your own goodness and pride

You will resent the fact that you rejected your chances at receiving the truth to believe a mirage, a lie

When it's too late, you'll realize that if your goodness can get you to Heaven, then Jesus suffered, died and bodily arose all in vain

But, the good news is, if you're able to read this, and God's speaking to your heart, you can accept the truth, and shun hell, and the splendors of Heaven, gain!

Consider the following, from God's Holy Word:

"For all have sinned, and come short of the glory of God; Being justified freely by his grace through the redemption that is in Christ Jesus: Whom God hath set forth to be a propitiation through faith in his blood, to declare his righteousness for the remission of sins that are past, through the forbearance of God." Romans 3:23-25

"For whosoever shall call upon the name of the Lord shall be saved." Romans 10:13

"Look unto me and be ye saved, all the ends of the earth: for I am God, and there is none else." Isaiah 45:22

SOMEONE ELSE

You may have everyone fooled, even your own self, believing that you're saved, even your spouse
But, there's Someone Who knows all and sees all! So, remember that Someone Else!

You may have no one in this world to turn to, for comfort and love
But, if you turn to Jesus, He gives peace, comfort and love from Heaven above!

You may have no help, and the way may seem bleak and dim
But, if you talk about it to that Someone Else, He will be your Guiding Light, within!

You may own very little in this ole' world, and struggle to make ends meet
But, when you're born again, you gain a mansion in Heaven, passed the gates of pearl,
    alongside the walls of jasper, beyond the crystal sea and The Throne of God is within
    walking distance, down the golden street!

Gods' Word: "Be not deceived; God is not mocked: for whatsoever a man soweth, that shall he
    also reap." Galatians 6:7

PASSED UP CHANCES
JOHN 4:6-14, REVELATION 14:11 & 21:8

Surely, the souls being cast into the lake of fire will look back into their lives, and take several
    glances
Surely, they'll see how Jesus reached out to them, offering to be their way to Heaven, and that
    they passed up many chances
Those souls will regret having felt Jesus' pleading during their lives, and choosing to ignore
All because they turned their backs on Jesus will they be tormented, as they burn forevermore
As they're horrified by being in an inescapable hell
Surely, they'll wish they'd of drank from The Living Well
Just as sure as the smoke of their torment will rise forever
They'll wish they could turn back the hands of time, but that'll happen NEVER!!

WILL YOU BE THERE?

JOHN 14:1-6 & REVELATION CHAPTERS 21 & 22

I care about you more than you know
And, I'm concerned about your soul, where one day it will go
Since I've learned the truth from The Bible
I've noticed your repeated denial
How sad to know the truth and see someone you care about caught up in a lie
I can't force you to see the light, but I will at least try
I've learned that the purpose of Jesus was to pay our way to Heaven, with His sinless blood
And that we can't enter Heaven just because we try to be good
The mercy seat in Heaven demanded a payment for our sins to be made
And Jesus' blood has already paid
For us, He gave His all
The only condition is that on His Name, we believe and call
If we try to pay our own way, we are ignoring what He has done
There is no way into Heaven, without reliance on God's Son
Dear friend, If I die before you
Let me leave you to think on a question or two:
Will you be there to claim the mansion built in your name?
Will you be there, and escape hells' flame?
Will you be there, to walk on the golden streets, beside the crystal sea?
Will you be there, instead of in hell, for all eternity?
Will you be there, to see that there's no sun or moon because Jesus is The Light?
Will you be there, rather than in hell, where there's torment day and night?
Will you be there, in Heaven, where no one will shed a tear?
Will you be there, far away from hells' tormenting fear?
Will you be there, in the Land of eternal bliss?
Will you be there, or will you continue to resist?

Consider God's Words:

> "And the devil that deceived them was cast into the lake of fire and brimstone, where the beast and the false prophet are, and shall be tormented day and night for ever and ever." Revelation 20:10

> "And death and hell were cast into the lake of fire. This is the second death. And whosoever was not found written in the book of life was cast into the lake of fire." Revelation 20:14-15

> "I Jesus have sent mine angel to testify unto you these things in the churches. I am the root and the offspring of David, and the bright and morning star. And the Spirit and the bride say, Come. And let him that heareth say, Come. And let him that is athirst come. And whosoever will, let him take the water of life freely....Surely I come quickly..." Revelation 22:16-20

ARE YOU READY TO DIE?

Are you ready to die?

Have you made out a will?

Who will get your stuff?

Who will get your soul?

Where will it go?

INVENTORS, CREATORS AND AUTHORS

Look around, and you see gadgets galore, and their inventors

Who created these things, and invented things from cars to ovens, washing machines to can openers

Notice that artwork comes from artists

All buildings have builders

Songs come from song writers

All books have authors

The universe, the earth, with all the living creatures upon it share the same Maker

And, we are guaranteed to meet Him sooner or later!

"O COME, let us sing unto the Lord: let us make a joyful noise to the rock of our salvation. Let us come before his presence with thanksgiving, and make a joyful noise unto him with psalms. For the LORD is a great God, and a great King above all gods. In his hand are the deep places of the earth: the strength of the hills is his also. The sea is his, and he made it: and his hands formed the dry land. O come, let us worship and bow down: let us kneel before the LORD our maker." Psalms 95:1-6

JESUS LOVES ALL

JOHN 3:16

It doesn't matter if you're big and brawny, or if you're teeny-tiny, JESUS LOVES ALL!

It doesn't matter if your skin is black, yellow or white, or if you are wrong or right, JESUS LOVES ALL!

It doesn't matter if you're good or if you're bad, if you're happy or if you're sad, JESUS LOVES ALL!

It doesn't matter if you have little money or a lot, or what the label says in the clothes you bought, JESUS LOVES ALL!

It doesn't matter if you're mean or nice, or if you give good or bad advice, JESUS LOVES ALL!

It doesn't matter what your size, shape, thoughts and heart look like, or if your actions are rude or polite, JESUS LOVES ALL!

It doesn't matter if you're "religious" or if you're "atheist", JESUS LOVES ALL!

It doesn't matter if by being good enough, you're trying to "earn" your way to Heaven, or if you don't care about understanding God's plan of salvation, JESUS LOVES ALL!

BEWARE of assuming that just because JESUS LOVES ALL that you will for sure go to Heaven one day! KNOWING He loves YOU isn't enough!

Because He loves all, He suffered, was put to shame; He paid what our sins cost, on Calvary's cross!

Because He loves all, He gives us a free will, the chance to choose between Heaven and hell!

Because He loves all, He gently pleads with our souls, He doesn't force us to be saved, He leaves that decision for us to control!

Because He loves all, He paid our way in to Heaven, with His sinless blood He washes away our sin, BUT, He said that to claim this cleansing, we MUST be born again!

Only one thing does He require, for us to receive salvation, it is simply that we call on His Name to save us, and believe!

Jesus said He is The Way to Heaven, not earthly people, dead people, not self; He is the one and only way into Heaven!

Jesus said, "I am the door: by me if any man enter in, he shall be saved..." John 10:9

Jesus said, "Enter ye in at the strait gate: for wide is the gate, and broad is the way, that leadeth to destruction, and many there be which go in thereat: Because strait is the gate, and narrow is the way, which leadeth unto life, and few there be that find it." Matthew 7:13-14

"The LORD hath appeared of old unto me, saying, Yea, I have loved thee with an everlasting love: therefore with lovingkindness have I drawn thee." Jeremiah 31:3

JESUS, MY SAVIOUR

When you find something exciting and new
And it proves itself to you
What do you do?
You tell everyone you know
Planting seeds of information about it in their minds to grow
And hope that their skepticism about it will soon let go

That's how I feel about Jesus, my Saviour
He came into my heart, saved me, and changed my life and behavior
And, to me compared the world to a Place that's Greater
All YOU have to do is, in Him, believe
And open your heart, calling on Him, too, and receive
Salvation, peace, joy, forgiveness...and seeds
To plant where He says to

What have you got to lose?

Eternal damnation, worry of falling short of salvation, and blues

What have you to gain?

Salvation, a Home in Heaven, and an eternity free from sorrow and pain!

THE POWER OF CHOICE

Most people search to have control, to have power of some kind

People assume that if they're in charge, they'll have peace of mind

People make daily choices

They hear their inner power-questing voices

People wish they could achieve the control, the power they've worked so hard to own

But, most people don't realize the fact that one day the power they strode for will be all gone

Think for a moment, wouldn't you say that it's a powerful thing to control your ETERNAL destiny?

The greatest "power" of all is already owned by each of us, we just need to hear and believe

The fact is that people are either on their way to Heaven, or on their way to hell

There is no "riding the fence" and no last minute "wishing well"

We have the power, the free will, to REJECT or TURN TO Jesus, and ask Him to save us, either will affect our life, and our after-life

We'll either be regretful in hells' torments, or enjoying eternal life!

BEWARE, once YOUR last moment is up, it's TOO LATE to consider Jesus and ask to be "beamed up"

Take heed to God's Word:

"Seek ye the LORD while he may be found, call ye upon him while he is near." Isaiah 55:6

"Boast not thyself of to morrow; for thou knowest not what a day may bring forth" Proverbs 27:1

"Therefore be ye also ready; for in such an hour as ye think not the Son of man cometh." Matthew 24:44

"For what is your life? It is even a vapour, that appeareth for a little time, and then vanisheth away." James 4:14

"Strive to enter in at the strait gate: for many, I say unto you, will seek to enter in, and shall not be able. When once the master of the house is risen up, and hath shut to the door, and ye begin to stand without, and to knock at the door, saying, Lord, Lord, open to us; and he shall answer and say unto you, I know you not whence ye are." Luke 13:24,25

A LETTER FOR YOU

Have you ever received a letter from someone that got a hold of your heart and changed your life, and the very core of your being, your views, making you into the best person you could possibly be, even changing the course of your eternal destiny?

Well, I have, as many others! We are called Christians. This lovely letter is God's Holy Bible.

My friend, you may wish to know why it is so powerful...

Because it was written to mankind by God, our Creator.

In the Bible, you'll find that events were written thousands of years before they happened.

And, guess what...they all happened! Exactly as God said they would.

Not only are these documented in His Word, but also, in the archives of history!

Non-Christians even found God's Word to be 100% accurate!

God says what He means, and He means what He says!

And, He is waiting for you, too, to read His letter to YOU.

Won't you see what He desires to say to your heart?

He created YOU, too, and He wants you to know what life and death are all about.

Would you like to live your life to it's fullest potential?

READ GOD'S LETTER TO YOU!

He gave you the very air that you breathe.

Surely, you'd like to learn about the purpose of your life, and what will happen after your death.

He knows when your last breath is...do you?

Don't spend it in regret.

Jesus, "Search the scriptures; for in them ye think ye have eternal life: and they are they which testify of me." John 5:39

TODAY IS THE DAY OF SALVATION

Accept Jesus today!

Do not delay

Or else you'll pay

Jesus is The Truth, The Life, The Way!

If you gamble with your soul, you will lose, and feel deep regret

You will burn eternally, rather than have everlasting life; on this truth, you can "bet"

What Jesus has to offer is so appealing!

Why reject Him, and not be receiving?

Just kneel, confessing that you need Him to save your soul, to cleanse you from all your sins...

And rise, having been born again, on your way, FOR SURE, to Heaven!

"...behold, now is the accepted time; behold, now is the day of salvation." 2Corinthians 6:2

WHAT OUR WORLD NEEDS

What does this world really need?

A better economy? To build bigger and better industries?

More money?

More milk and honey?

More advanced technology?

More studies in biology?

If you guess kindness or world peace...

You're close, but missing the mark! The answer is:

More people turning to Jesus!

THE GREATEST STORY

My favorite story, the greatest of all time, is very exciting, and true

It is about this Man, Who was a Jew

He was a man in the flesh

But, through God and the virgin Mary, He was birthed

He performed miracles as He lived His life

And, He taught about God and salvation to every one is sight

Temptation He faced and defeated

God His Father was all that He needed

What is so interesting is that He carried His own cross

After being whipped, ridiculed, and beat beyond recognition, He walked to the mount He was
 to be hung upon

He suffered through tremendous pain

So that WE may have salvation

He rose from the dead after three days, to soon join His Father

And we're told in The Bible that if we believe this and ask Him to save our soul, then He will,
 and He'll ask His Father to be ours, too!

MY FRIEND
PROVERBS 18:24 & JOHN 3:3

Have you ever had a friend to answer your every call to come and be with you in the middle of
 the night, right away?

Have you ever had a friend that can give you perfect advice for every aspect of your life?

Have you ever had a friend that forgives and forgets every single thing you've done wrong to
  them in the past?

Have you ever had a friend that follows you everywhere you go, to be sure that you're safe?

Have you ever had a friend catch your every tear, being ever near?

Have you ever had a friend that guarantees to keep every single promise they've ever made to you?

Have you ever had a friend that has the power to move mountains?

I have a Friend that does ALL this, and SO MUCH more!!!

His Name is Jesus Christ.

Have you ever had a Friend that suffered and died for YOUR sins, that you may have
  forgiveness from God and live in Heaven forever?

You've got One!! All you have to do is turn to Him while He's calling, believe in faith, being
  born again!

WILL THEY GET THEIR CHANCE?

LUKE 2:13-14 & 15:10

When Jesus Christ was born on earth

A multitude of heavenly angels praised His birth

They were filled with joy, to see the start of redemptions' plan

They were praising God for sending a Saviour to man

Those angels waited a long time to see this scene unfold

The birth of Jesus, Who would die to save each mans' soul

Glory to God in the highest, their voices sang

As excitement and joy in them rang

Jesus said that God's angels are joyed with each soul that gets saved

And He said they have joy over each person who repents for how they have behaved

Think of the thief who hung on a cross

Who turned to and trusted Jesus

What joy the angels must of had

When they saw the salvation of a man who was bad

Think of the guard at the prison, where Paul and Silas were cast in

Through their witness for Jesus, he turned from his sin

What joy the angels had as he asked how to be saved

What rejoicing the angels did, when his family did the same

Think of the woman at the well

Who met Jesus and got saved, before she died in her sins and went to hell

What joy filled Heavens' angels, as she became honest with The Lord
What rejoicing they had that her life was changed forevermore
Think about the apostle Paul, who was steeped in religion
In God's Name, he persecuted the Christians
What joy the angels had as he was changed on the Damascus Road
What rejoicing took place in Heaven, when he arose

Think about your soul, and the choice YOU have to make
The decision is YOURS, YOU control your own fate
The angels hear Gods' Still, Small Voice speaking to YOUR heart
Will they get their chance to rejoice over your salvation, or will they sadly depart?

Luke 2:13-14, "And suddenly there was with the angel a multitude of the heavenly host praising
     God, and saying, Glory to God in the highest, and on earth peace, good will toward men."
Luke 15:10, Jesus speaking, "Likewise, I say unto you, there is joy in the presence of the angels
     of God over one sinner that repenteth."

WHY HOLD BACK?

God has placed a precious package somewhere in your life
And, sadly, you don't look to open it until you are desperate and overcome with strife
Not only does this gift contain salvation
But, also is peace of mind, constant comfort, forgiveness, and answers to life's questions
God has placed in this gift: room for YOU at the cross of Christ, the blood that Jesus shed to
     save us
All you have to do is accept this gift, to go to Heaven, it is a MUST!
Those who toss this gift aside, this question I ask:
Why are you holding back?
Who, in their right mind would pass up the chance to go to Heaven?
And choose a destiny, that ends in the lake of fire; shunning God's love, forgiveness and salvation!?

ONE OR THE OTHER

As we go through daily life, we face decisions, small and great
But, the one usually paid the least attention to making is the one that controls our fate!
We're so concerned about living life that we give death no thought
Think about it, how long is our life when compared to eternity? The way to Heaven, have you
     diligently sought?

Let God's Word be your "roadmap" to salvation, to Heaven
Read it! Study it! Pray over it! Don't depend on man-made religion and tradition!
What man makes cannot last forever! But what God says will stand forever!
Modern science even proves that we had an "Intelligent Creator", historians cannot prove God's
    Word to be in error. What God's Word predicts WILL happen, just like so many times before!
God's Word says that each soul will go to Heaven or hell, with no way of escape! Too bad
    people ignore this pressing decision, focusing on everything else under the sun!
Why do grandparents, parents, siblings, friends reject going to one Place, to end up in another?

REJOICE

When you are sad
Know that there's plenty reason to be glad!
Just let your soul receive what you can have...
An everlasting relationship with Jesus, our Creator! By trusting in Him as your Saviour
He will wash away the sins of your past, and change your behavior

And, when your tears are falling
Know that He is always there, waiting for your calling
Just let Him in your heart and He will keep it from "stalling"
When you have no one to comfort you
Know that God will, if you allow Him to
Just call on Him, and what you need from Him, He will do
When you do not know how to keep from having a bad day
Know that God will show you the way
He is always just a prayer away
So, drop to your knees and bow your head
And think about the wonderful things, through the Bible He said
And know that anything negative that may come your way, with Him, you don't have to dread
He is a wonderful Saviour and Friend
Get saved TODAY, and He'll be with you even after "the end"

IF I EVER COME UP MISSING

To all of my friends, loved ones, acquaintances, and known or unknown foes...
I have some news to share, that you must know
If I ever come up missing, and cannot be found, not even my body-deceased
Let me tell you where I'll be...

I will be in Glory with Jesus!

I will be dwelling in The Place He prepared for the saved, the righteous

Faith in Jesus changed me, as well as my destiny, by just believing that He died and now lives

Faith in His finished work covers me in His blood, I'll be forever known as "His"

Let me share from first Thessalonians chapter four, verse seventeen some news, God's Word...

"Then we which are alive and remain shall be caught up together with them in the clouds, to
     meet The Lord in the air: and so shall we ever be with the Lord."

This, readers, is called the "rapture"

And, if you're NOT saved you won't be called up, what a DISASTER!

EVEN IF LIFE'S GOOD

If you have all the goodness this world offers

If you've achieved your goals, your health is good, you're sailing on smooth waters

If you have a beautiful home, nice belongings, a loving family

If you have all your heart desires, you're satisfied, having plenty of money

If you sum your life up as being good

Even YOU have a need, which is to prepare for death, as all of us should

Even YOU need a Saviour, because of your sin

Even YOU have a hell to shun and a Heaven to win

The goodness of this life doesn't carry over to eternity

When it comes down to your bare soul, Jesus asks, "What have YOU done with Me?"

Can you say that you called on Him to be saved, as we all should?

Or, will your reply be, "I didn't need You, because my life was good."??

God's Word says:

   "Forasmuch as ye know that ye were not redeemed with corruptible things, as silver and gold,
   from your vain conversation received by tradition from your fathers; But with the precious
   blood of Christ, as of a lamb without blemish and without spot"   1Peter 1:18-19

   Jesus, "For what is a man profited, if he shall gain the whole world, and lose his own soul?
   what shall a man give in exchange for his soul? Matthew 16:26

WHAT'S THE REASON WHY?

INSPIRED BY CONVERSATIONS WITH UNSAVED PEOPLE
AND MY OWN MEMORIES OF ONCE THINKING LIKE THIS

Many people call on The Lord for something

Many call out to Him in vain

They ask God for help to change, or for help with a decision

Some cry out to Him for wisdom

Many sincerely call, meaning well

And, because they've asked Him for this or that, they think they'll one day avoid hell

A scared child can ask God to calm their fears

They can continuously ask Him for strength, throughout the years

And when they're grown, they feel as though He heard and answered

But, sadly, most don't know of His salvation, and can't quote one verse of scripture

They think they know all they need to know about God, because once upon a time they called
     on Him in desperation

And, they miss salvation!

It's good to call out to God when we're hurting or grieved

But, to get into Heaven one day, this isn't the key

We need to come to the point, when God deals with our heart, showing us that we sin

That we realize because of our sin, we cannot enter Heaven

For this, did Jesus come to earth, to bleed, die and arise!

He saw our need and paid the price!

When we call on Him for forgiveness, asking for pardon, for salvation

He sees if we're sincere, and if we are, He refuses no one!

My friend, there is a difference in asking God for help with problems, and in asking Him to
     save your soul from hell

You'd be wise to open your heart and consider things well

When you've called on God, what was the reason why?

Was it for Him to save your soul? Or to help you in this life get by?

Consider God's Word:

> "In whom we have redemption through his blood, the forgiveness of sins, according to the
> richness of his grace" Ephesians 1:7

> "Tell ye, and bring them near; yea, let them take counsel together: who hath declared this
> from ancient time: who hath told it from that time? have not I the LORD? and there is no
> God else beside me; a just God and a Saviour; there is none beside me. Look unto me, and be
> ye saved, all the ends of the earth: for I am God, and there is none else." Isaiah 45:21-22

SUCH A HAPPY PLACE
REVELATION CHAPTERS 21 &22

How exciting, to think about Heaven, my sweet Home some day

How thrilled I am to be going! Thank You, Jesus, for being The Way!

I've been reading about how beautiful it will be there, with the streets of gold, the jasper walls, the gates of giant pearl, the glory of Jesus, ever shining

The glorious rainbow over God's throne, the angelic host, The Saviour of my soul, hearing the saved ones all eternally singing

Land of no more tears, sorrow or pain

Clear skies, a gentle breeze, no need for rain

The Book of Life, my bottled tears, the face of God looking upon even me

Singing, whistling, friendships, peace for all eternity

The sea as crystal, the Tree of Life, Moses, Abraham, Joseph, Noah

Jacob, Isaac, Esther, Ruth, Boaz, even Jonah!

John the Baptist, the Apostle Paul, John the Beloved, Joseph the Carpenter

Peter, James, Lazarus, Mary, the Philippian Jailor

Timothy, the folks at Galatia, Ephesus, Philippi

All the saved folks through the ages, oh my!

Spurgeon, Mueller, Torrey, Wesley, Whitefield, Moody

Edwards, Oswald Chambers, Tozer and others, to talk with for all eternity!

My dear Christian friends

Missionaries that obeyed when God sent

The sweet lady and loving old man from the rest home

All the aborted babies, miscarried babies, toddlers and infants that passed on, are all around God's throne!

The silver saints that smiled as they departed from this world

The preachers galore, that stood for, "Thus saith The Lord"

Those that stood in the gap, praying for my soul

The Good Shepherd who takes good care of His fold!

Oh, Heaven is such a happy place

I'm so glad I'm as good as already there, thanks to God's saving grace!

Of all those named, will you be there, in this happy place?

Or will you continue rejecting God's saving grace?

THEY WILL WISH THEY WOULD OF SAID YES TO JESUS

Oh, the countless souls that will be burning in the lake of fire, being choked on the smoke of
their own torment

Surely, they'll all be wishing that to Heaven they went

They will be thinking back, as they suffer, wishing they would of listened to the witness of
others, wishing that they would of read the gospel tracts that once were in their hand

But, it's too late! They're in this place of darkness, separated from God forever! They'll never
see "That Fair Land"

When they're hoping the torments will be done...

They'll realize that eternity has just begun!

Surely for all of eternity, they'll be full of regret!

They will be wishing that to Jesus they'd of said, "Yes!"

Take heed of the warnings:

> "And the sea gave up the dead which were in it; and death and hell delivered up the dead
> which were in them: and they were judged every man...And death and hell were cast into the
> lake of fire. This is the second death. And whosoever was not found written in the book of
> life was cast into the lake of fire."
>
> -Revelation 20:13-14

> "And the smoke of their torment ascendeth up for ever and ever..." -Revelation 14:11

HOW TO GET TO HEAVEN

Avoid distractions, open your heart to God, to His way, the ONLY way

If you are not **totally, 100%** sure you will go to Heaven, if you were to die this day

Consider that even you are a sinner, as Romans 3:23 says, "For all have sinned and come short
of the glory of God."

Realize that because we sin, our penalty is death and hell, Romans 6:23, "For the wages of sin
is death..."

"And death and hell were cast into the lake of fire...And whosoever was not found written in
the book of

life was cast into the lake of fire." -Revelation 20:14-15

Acknowledge that Jesus paid the penalty for our sins, on the cross, Romans 5:8, "But God
commendeth his love toward us, in that, while we were yet sinners, Christ died for us."

Listen for The Lord, speaking to your heart, telling you this is all true. Don't reject His gentle plea!

Know that if you ask God to forgive your sin, and if you receive Jesus Christ, God will save your
soul, Romans, 10:13, "For whosoever shall call upon the name of the Lord shall be saved."

Talk to God, out loud, and tell Him that you acknowledge you're a sinner. Tell him that you know Jesus died on the cross for YOU. Ask Him to forgive you and to come into your heart and save your soul.

Be assured that God will hear you! Jesus said, in John 6:37, "him that cometh to me I will in no wise cast out."

Trust what God has done for you! Rest assured that He will take you to Heaven, for you coming His way, not trying to get there by trying to be good enough! Jesus, His Son is the way!

Rely on God's promise, Romans 10:9-10, " If thou shalt confess with thy mouth the Lord Jesus, and shalt believe in thine heart that God hath raised him from the dead, thou shalt be saved. For with the heart man believeth unto righteousness; and with the mouth confession is made unto salvation."

ON MY WAY TO HEAVEN, THEN WHAT?

Tell others! Let them know what great thing God has done for you! Let Jesus know you are not ashamed of Him, by telling others about your salvation! Jesus says in Matthew 10:32, "Whosoever therefore shall confess me before men, him will I confess also before my Father which is in heaven."

Know that you will sin in the future, but that doesn't take away your salvation. When you do sin, do as 1John 1:9 says, "If we confess our sins, he is faithful and just to forgive us our sins, and to cleanse us from all unrighteousness."

Familiarize yourself with God's Holy Word, as in Psalms 119:11 & 15, "Thy word have I hid in my heart...I will meditate in thy precepts, and have respect unto thy ways."

Go to a church that teaches according to what The Bible says about how to obtain salvation, Hebrews 10:25, "Not forsaking the assembling of ourselves together.."

Compare what they say to what God says, when visiting churches and looking for the right one, "Study to shew thyself approved unto God, a workman that needeth not to be ashamed, rightly dividing the word of truth."

Be baptized as scripture says, this does not cleanse from sin, but is for a testimony of already having been saved, Romans 6:4, "Therefore we are buried with him by baptism into death: that like as Christ was raised up from the dead by the glory of the Father, even so we also should walk in newness of life."

Serve God according to His Word and His leading in your heart, Mark 16:15, Jesus, "..Go ye into all the world, and preach the gospel to every creature." Preach here means to tell; to share by means of speaking.

Be not ashamed, as in Romans 10:11, "For the scripture saith, Whosoever believeth on him shall not be ashamed."

Chapter Ten

Pathway of Quick Reflections

I will instruct thee and teach thee in the way which thou shalt
go: I will guide thee with mine eye.   Psalm 32:8

LITTLE SAYINGS FOR CHRISTIANS

Stay close to The Lord, that you may be calm before the storm!

The Lord owns you, have you acknowledged this fact yet?

Alongside the road to sin, have you noticed the warning signs?

Jesus best protects those who show Him no neglect!

You can't drift away if you're anchored!

When you love Jesus, you can't help but show it!

Secure the entrance of your mind daily with reading and prayer; this makes it harder for satan
   to get through!

The more I learn, the more I yearn to see my Saviour face to face!

Life's race: it ain't over 'til the trumpet sounds, unless God chooses to bring you home first!
   Witness while you can!

Lacking the fullness of God? Don't be a malnutritioned Christian! Feast on His Word!

If it doesn't bring Jesus treasure, it should not be your treasure!

Get with God regularly, because the flesh is weak!

Our life's not about us, it's about Jesus!

From the depths of the valleys, we can see the height of the mountains; thank God for them!

To see things with the right perspective, bow down low!

The world loses it charm when in God's family you're born!

Let's obey our Father, like good little children!

The farther we go from Jesus, the more we need Him!

Get your Daddy, if the battle's too hard!

Complaining brings glory to your problem, not your Lord!

God's available 365 days a year; and even when it's leap year!

Get with God when you must make decisions!

Treat others as you would treat Jesus, He said to do all as unto Him!

Don't just look the part, have the heart!

I'll be okay, because Jesus is with me!

Work at home: Serve The Lord! The benefits are worth it!

Remember to walk by faith, not by sight!

Put on the whole armour of God!

If you're seeking to win the lost, share your Saviour with them, not your convictions. Once they meet Him, He will give them convictions.

Always seek to point everyone around you to Jesus!

Talk much about your blessings, and you'll talk less about your problems, and God will receive more glory!

Listening to gossip is just as bad as speaking it!

I want people to rejoice at my funeral! Trust me, I'll be rejoicing!

Try to make your reflection look like Jesus'.

Thank God constantly!

Remember that thanks makes praise easy!

Witness your own death, as you die to self daily!

When drifting down the river of loneliness and grief, look to Jesus, standing on the bank. He'll deliver you!

Make the time to just plain enjoy God!

We'll be praising God for all eternity, why not practice now?

Be honored to serve God!

It's hard to work for The Lord when your spirit is smothered by unconfessed sin!

Our actions follow our words, oh, be careful little lips what you say!

When you're wrong, just admit it!

Ask God to show you what to want in life.

Make a habit to forgive others as quick as possible!

Don't just tell Jesus you love Him, prove it!

Jesus bought us, and promised to never ask for a refund!

When Jesus bought me, He got an ole' fixer upper! May I take pleasure in the changes He makes in me!

Tell The Lord what you know He already knows, "I love You", etc.

Build everything in your life on the foundation of Jesus!

Pass on godly traits to your children!

Be in one accord with God's other children!

Remember to try every spirit!

Seek to be found faithful to the end!

Try to keep your words as fresh as you try to keep your breath.

Give sin a bad name before it gives you a bad name!

Respect the property of others. This includes those Whom God owns!

When the fiery dart of self pity comes at you, be sure to duck!

The most rewarding job is serving Jesus!

Run your race as though Jesus is waiting at the finish line for you. He is!

Don't be a lazy, sloppy, rebellious Christian!

Who should have control, the Artist, or the paint brush?

Polish your life, that it may shine for Jesus.

Observe how you affect others, if it's not drawing them closer to God, make some changes.

Be all that you can be, to the glory of God!

Get on your knees before The Lord, He can thaw out your cold heart!

Christians are meant to go against the grain!

Give Jesus your all, I mean your ALL!

Our words are like a sword, they can hurt others, or cut through the dark, that God's light may shine through!

Don't be surprised if you hear, "Come up hither" today, Jesus said to expect it!

Sin swallows our faith like quicksand!

Treat pride like the plague! It is!

Are you bearing the fruit of The Spirit, or the fruit of sin?

Cause others to be curious to know more about your Lord, brag on Him!

Show the devil that you aren't his! Prove to him that you belong to Jesus!

Don't be too proud to ask your Father for help!

Sin is like a pot-hole, avoid as many as possible.

We're one day closer to Heaven!

God's prescription for our ailments: Thanks, Prayer, Joy, Faith, Praise, The Bible.

The Bible is my daily multivitamin!

We look like a bulls' eye to satan! Be aware!

Take care of what you sew, you have to reap it one day!

Pull up to the pump of God's Word and say, "Filler' up!"

Learn from your trials, and others'.

Don't just seek to be average!

When satan tempts you, tell him, "I'll take Jesus, thank you!"

Shame on you, if God did something for you and you didn't tell anyone about it!

When God gives us talents, He intends for us to use them to bring Him glory.

We are always teaching our children. What do we teach them the most? What was today's lesson?

Daily drink the milk of God's Word, so that you won't be spiritually stunted!

Let Jesus love others through you.

Try to be a better Christian today than you were yesterday. Try to be a better Christian tomorrow than you are today.

Let others know that you appreciate them!

Pray the most for those you like the least! Now, this will exercise your faith!

Christians ought to hide God's Word in their hearts.

Don't condemn those serving God! You're just upset that what they're doing makes you look that much lazier.

Let your daily motto be: GIVE GOD THE GLORY!

When you trip over your flesh, get back up!

LITTLE SAYINGS TO THOSE NOT YET SAVED

God did create us. Don't wait until you meet Him to believe it.

God's Word says that one day every knee will bow to Him, you'd be better off if you bow now!

Jesus is real! Don't wait to see His face to find out!

When you are ready to die, then you are ready to live!

One day, all of Heaven will be singing to The Lord. There will be no singing in hell! There, there's only screaming!

Read your Bible to find out about eternal survival.

Don't close your eyes to the light of the gospel.

Prepare for eternity NOW, when you're there, it will be TOO LATE!

You may be just one heartbeat away from death, call on Jesus now!

Don't follow your heart, it could deceive you! Follow Gods' Word, it's been proven!

The traditions of men and their religion do not get anyone to Heaven!

Even doctors need a doctor, counselors need a counselor, and those unsaved need The Saviour!

There will be no homeless souls in eternity, they will be either living in Heaven or hell, what about you?

Jesus is reaching his nail-pierced hands out to YOU, don't reject them!

Prepare for eternity, you never know when you'll meet it face to face!

If eternity scares you, chances are good that you need Jesus!

If you tell yourself that you don't need Jesus to get to Heaven, you're really convincing yourself to go to hell!

Religion keeps more people out of Heaven, than it teaches them to get in! Religion is a stumbling stone! You need Jesus, not religion!

Those who ignore Jesus will one day be on their knees screaming out to Him for help, but then will be too late, their choice will have already been made!

Those who call God's children Jesus freaks obviously aren't God's children.

One day, we will see the evil spirits that attack us. Hopefully, it won't consist of us spending eternity with them!

If you want to meet the saints some day, don't count on them to get you to Heaven, Jesus is the only way!

When Jesus calls you, don't hesitate, it may be too late!

Don't wait until you're in eternity to decide where you want to go-you must choose now, God said!

Choosing to ignore being saved is choosing to spend eternity in hell.

Jesus loves you, won't you come to Him?

Jesus paid your way into Heaven; trying to pay on your own gets you no admission! Trust in Him!

What if you plan to be saved in two days, but die tomorrow? You've gambled with your soul and lost!

Forever is a long time! Wouldn't you like to spend it in Heaven? Say yes to Jesus today!

My Pastor has graciously agreed to my request to supply readers with a way of contact. If you need any further help, or have a question about how to be saved and sure of Heaven, please contact:

Pastor Howard Owens
Amazing Grace Baptist Church
(Independent)
(336) 573-2909